THE INGREDIENTS OF
GREAT COOKING

—*Thousands of years of dependence on a basically non-meat diet to provide balanced nutrition.*

—*Cooking methods that insure the preservation of natural flavors, vitamins, and food fibers.*

—*A reverence for the sanctity of the humblest foods.*

—*An aesthetic sense that makes cooking an art—a harmonious blending of color, taste, and texture to provide sensuous pleasure.*

All have combined to produce the succulent triumphs to be found from

CHINESE
MEATLESS
COOKING

ABOUT THE AUTHOR: STELLA LAU FESSLER was born in Hong Kong, where she studied Chinese cooking for several years in a school for professional cooks, as she later was to study French cuisine in Paris. Currently she divides her time between lecturing in Chinese at Cornell University and conducting a near-legendary course in Chinese cooking in her own home.

CHINESE MEATLESS COOKING

Revised and Updated

STELLA LAU FESSLER

ILLUSTRATED BY
JANET NELSON

A SIGNET BOOK

NEW AMERICAN LIBRARY

TIMES MIRROR

NAL BOOKS ARE AVAILABLE AT QUANTITY DISCOUNTS
WHEN USED TO PROMOTE PRODUCTS OR SERVICES. FOR
INFORMATION PLEASE WRITE TO PREMIUM MARKETING
DIVISION, THE NEW AMERICAN LIBRARY, INC., 1633
BROADWAY, NEW YORK, NEW YORK 10019.

SIGNET, SIGNET CLASSICS, MENTOR, PLUME, MERIDIAN AND
NAL BOOKS are published by The New American Library, Inc.,
1633 Broadway, New York, New York 10019

First Signet Printing, June, 1983

1 2 3 4 5 6 7 8 9

PRINTED IN THE UNITED STATES OF AMERICA

CONTENTS

ACKNOWLEDGMENTS

My grateful thanks to Professor and Mrs. Theodore J. Lowi for their invaluable aid in introducing me to the publishing world, and to my agent Maryanne Colas, who had faith in my book and the patience to find a publisher. I am indebted to Paul Cheng and Ni Tseh, whose expert help at Cornell's Olin Library made the research task much simpler. My particular thanks to Gerald Howard, my editor, for his expert guidance throughout; his enthusiasm for and understanding of vegetarian cooking did so much to improve my book.

I am grateful to my cousin, Lincoln Lin, for providing information on the mail order spots in the San Francisco area; to my husband, John McCoy, for reading the entire draft and giving priceless suggestions and valuable advice; to my son, Freeman Fessler, for sampling all the food tested in this book with his sharp palate and good appetite.

Finally, special thanks to all my students through the years, whose interest and enthusiasm have encouraged me to write a cookbook.

INTRODUCTION

Those close to the court get honor,
those close to the kitchen get food.

—*Chinese folk saying*

There have been countless cookbooks written on the culinary art of China and on the various cuisines of every region in China. However the school of Buddhist vegetarian cookery seems to have been neglected. A category so unique and important is definitely worth recognition equal to those that have already been extensively praised. The greatness of Chinese cuisines cannot be completely appreciated without sampling vegetarian cookery. In this sense my book serves as a supplement to the variety of Chinese cookbooks already published.

Because meat has never been the main source of protein for the Chinese, for thousands of years they have been relying on non-meat foodstuffs to provide most of the nutrition in their diet. For that reason, cooking with vegetarian ingredients is indeed the foundation of all the sophisticated cuisines of China. China has long been a predominantly agricultural country with very little emphasis on raising livestock. People have depended on foods that come directly from the soil. In addition, Buddhism and Taoism have had great influence on the Chinese diet. In the teachings of Buddhism there are five abstentions. One of them is an injunction against taking life. Killing any living being is considered a crime of varying degrees, depending on the creature killed. In Taoist belief, meat is unclean; thus, in order to purify the blood, meat is forbidden by their dietary laws. Since eating meat is against the orthodox teachings of these two religions, the major source of protein for their adherents has been vegetables. All these factors place great stress on vegetarian culinary skills, and as a result have helped create a unique art of vegetarian cooking.

I remember those wonderful and delectably displayed vegetarian meals that I have eaten in Chinese monasteries and restaurants in Hong Kong: ten-course banquets with mock meat and mock fish dishes that not only looked exactly like fish, chicken, duck, sausage, and tripe but tasted deliciously similar to the real thing. Each of these dishes had its own well-known name, such as Mock Roast Duck or Buddha's Chicken. There were also vegetable dishes with poetic names referring to temples, monks, nuns, and immortals. In cooking Buddhist meals, one has to improvise with limited materials to reconstruct artful dishes that look and taste like chicken, fish, etc. It requires great imagination, an artistic mind, and fantastic ingenuity. To a Chinese cook, imitating a certain meat dish with non-meat ingredients is not simply a matter of replacing the meat. It is instead an effort to show off the great culinary art of China, to make the impossible possible.

Chinese vegetarians range from complete to partial in their degrees of rejection of meat and meat products in the diet. Some pure vegetarians will not touch any meat or any food that has been cooked with meat; some will eat fish but not animal meat; some will include eggs in their diet but not seafood. Besides the monks and the nuns who are full-time vegetarians for ethical reasons, there are also laymen who are committed to a completely meatless diet for spiritual reasons as well. Some believe that by not eating meat one is purifying one's soul. Others want to accumulate merit for their afterlives. There are also some who turn vegetarian as penance. Then there are the occasional vegetarians who for any of the above reasons may abstain from meat on special days, such as New Year's, or the first and the fifteenth of each lunar month.

Recent years have seen the spread of interest in vegetarianism in the Western world. Young people in particular are experimenting with vegetarian diets for reasons of health, economy, or self-discipline. Much has been written about the future problems of world overpopulation and food shortages. It seems clear that vegetable foods, particularly high-protein vegetables, will play an expanding role in counteracting the increased costs and reduced availability of meat. One goal of this book is to make such a shift more interesting and more palatable.

A NOTE ON NUTRITION

Since dairy products are not commonly used by the Chinese, one may wonder how the Chinese vegetarian obtains a balanced diet. In the book *Diet for a Small Planet*, Mrs. Frances Moore Lappé has put together some excellent recipes and given us a number of formulas for mixing different plant proteins together to obtain a protein-balanced diet. The Chinese, in fact, have been doing for centuries exactly what Mrs. Lappé recommended in her book. As most people know, the Chinese eat a mixed-and-matched meal. A typical Chinese family meal consists of eggs, bean curd, vegetables, and a small amount of meat or seafood. Never does one single kind of meat or vegetable dominate the entire meal. As a result, their chopsticks are constantly darting from one dish to another, taking a little bit from this dish and then a little bit from that. The foods that they eat complement each other in taste and texture and also provide the necessary proteins for their bodies.

As a matter of fact, a great deal of the advice that we get from most of the scientific dietary books today matches the way the Chinese have been eating all along. Let us look at the recent research on high-fiber diet. Many doctors consider that a high-fiber diet can decrease diseases such as colonic cancer and heart attack. In her book *The Natural High-Fiber Life Saving Diet*, Ms. Subak-Sharp has shown us through her extensive research the importance of natural fiber in our diet. If we look at the way the Chinese cook their vegetables and the amount they consume, it corroborates Ms. Subak-Sharp's research perfectly. In other words the Chinese diet is also a healthy diet high in natural fiber content. It is not just the use of vegetables themselves, but more particularly the way they are cooked. By Western standards Chinese vegetables are undercooked, but it is this minimal cooking that preserves the fiber content and increases the nutritional value of the dish.

You may also notice that about half of the recipes in this book call for one kind of soybean product or another. Soybeans have been the essential source of protein for the Chinese for thousands of years. According to a United States Department of Agriculture report, a pound of dried soybeans contains 154.7 grams of protein, whereas a pound of beef may have only 95 to 99 grams of protein. Soybeans are also extremely low in calories and contain no saturated fats. In addition to using soybeans in their original form, the Chinese also transform them into soybean milk, soy sauce, bean curd, pressed bean curd cakes, plain bean curd sheets, and er-ju bean curd sheets, and so on. Foods like bean curd (tofu, pronounced do'fu), solidified with calcium sulfate, are rich in calcium. Other bean curd forms—for example, deep-fried bean curd puffs, pressed bean curd cakes, frozen bean curd, bean curd sheets, and er-ju bean curd sheets—are very high in minerals such as iron, phosphorus, and potassium. All these varieties of soybean products give the Chinese considerable amounts of protein, minerals, and vitamins.

In this book I have provided recipes that use many varieties of Chinese soybean products. All of them are delicious, nutritious, and easy to make. To all those who love good food but live just a bit too far away from a Chinese monastery for a vegetarian meal, I present this book.

BASICS OF
CHINESE COOKING

*Drink and eat moderately and carefully,
and garden vegetables can be like
feasting on rich delicacies.*

—"Master Chu's mottoes for
guiding the family" (Ching Dynasty)

Before one begins to do Chinese cooking, one must first under-
stand the Chinese attitude toward food. Food has always been
a basic comfort and source of enjoyment for the Chinese,
whose living conditions have traditionally been harsh. In a land
where the need for food is desperate, anything that can cure
hunger becomes precious. For the Chinese nothing edible
should be wasted; every single grain of rice is produced
through toil and suffering; therefore it is sacred, as precious as
pearls.

Hunger and natural disaster were certainly not unique to
China, so we cannot use these factors alone to explain why
cooking developed into a fine art in that culture. The historical
evidence of other great cuisines around the world indicates that
in ancient Rome and later in Italy and France, the art form was
developed just as in China by that social class least likely to be
affected by famine and food shortages. These aristocratic
classes had the wealth, the leisure, and the inclination to develop and support the art, and haute cuisine arose fortuitously
in several places as a response to an interest by the upper class.
Yet certainly the unique features of Chinese cuisine were affected by the special conditions of all of Chinese life. The fact
that nothing edible escaped the peasant's attention contributed
to the magnificent variety found on the tables of the Chinese

aristocrats. Also, there is no question that the constant specter of famine influenced the thinking and the emotions of the Chinese upper classes even though they were least touched by such disasters.

The lack of fuel, too, undoubtedly played a major role in shaping the cuisine of China. Cooking methods such as stir-frying and steaming food in the same pot with the rice were originally developed to conserve fuel; meanwhile, sophisticated contrasts of flavors were discovered and innovative cooking skills were created.

The gastronomic aspects of Chinese culture developed over a period of about three thousand years, and today the cooking methods and eating habits still remain more or less the same. The distinctive character of Chinese cooking, as it differs from the Western style, lies in its unique emphasis on the blending of flavors and variations of texture that require inventive culinary preparation. In most Western-style cooking meat is quite often prepared in large pieces and vegetables are cooked separately. But in Chinese cooking the ingredients are first cut up into small pieces in various shapes, and vegetables and meat are cooked together to improve flavors and provide textural contrasts. Moreover, the Chinese way of dining is communal; they share the different dishes with all the diners around the table. People of Western cultures may do the same at home, but in public they are more likely to order a single individual dish and not share in the variety that may be available around the table. Often when dining in Chinese restaurants I have noticed Western parties ordering individual dishes which each member treated as his personal dinner. This Western style of ordering is totally inappropriate to a Chinese meal. It not only means that each individual denies himself the variety offered by sharing, but also leads the beginner to hesitate to experiment for fear he would be stuck with a single dish that he did not like.

CUTTING METHODS

In Chinese cooking most vegetables and meat are cut up before being cooked. The ingredients are cut into various shapes according to the nature and appearance of each dish. This step serves two obviously useful purposes. One is to cut down on the amount of time required for cooking, thus saving fuel in a country where it has always been at a premium. Another is that it makes it possible for the Chinese to use chopsticks as practical eating utensils.

I am one who believes in ad-libbing in cooking. I think one should learn to improvise with whatever is available, to create a delicious dish or even a whole meal. If you have a reasonably sharp knife in the kitchen you can start your cutting and whip up an authentic Chinese dish in no time. However, if you are planning to stock your kitchen with a new knife, I would suggest that you invest in a Chinese all-purpose kitchen knife—the cleaver, a most versatile implement. Almost every part of the cleaver can be used to do something: the sharp blade for cutting ingredients into various shapes and sizes; the blunt side of the blade for pounding and mashing, serving as a meat hammer; the broad side of the cleaver for smashing and crushing ingredients such as ginger and garlic and for sweeping up cut-up food and transporting it to pan or plate; and the end of the wooden handle for grinding peppercorns or crushing fermented black beans, serving as a pestle. The Chinese cleaver comes in several sizes, but if you are buying just one, choose a heavier and larger one. The weight helps the blade glide through the material faster, requiring less exertion from the cook. A heavy cleaver also gives weight for mincing and chopping. Cleavers are made of either tempered carbon steel or stainless steel; if you are buying just one, get carbon steel because the metal is softer and can be more easily sharpened when it becomes dull. However, carbon steel rusts easily, so rinse and dry the cleaver thoroughly after each use. When the knife becomes rusty, scrub it with some scouring powder, rinse it thoroughly, and then coat the flat blade with a few drops of vegetable oil.

Although the cleaver looks like a deadly weapon, it is actually a most useful and marvelous tool when you know how it should be handled. An experienced cook is absolutely confident of his art in cutting, even when performing with dazzling speed with the cleaver. Though it seems dangerous to others, he knows that knives are not dangerous in themselves; it is simply up to him to command the blade to do what he wishes.

The following cutting methods assume the use of a Chinese cleaver. Except for pounding, mashing, and grinding, however, any kitchen knife can be used.

In using a cleaver, hold it in whichever hand you cut with, gripping the handle naturally and comfortably with about an inch of your thumb touching one side of the flat blade and half of your index finger bending slightly downward touching the other side of the flat blade; your thumb and the index

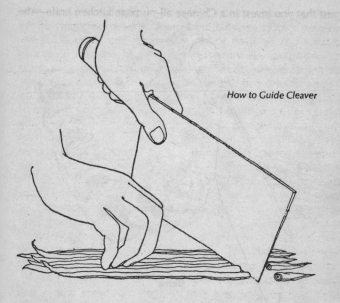

How to Guide Cleaver

finger should now be in control of the knife so you can manipulate it easily. The best position when cutting with the cleaver is to place the cutting board on a table or a kitchen counter at about the level of your waist. This position will provide you with a natural flow of force pressing down from the shoulder and the upper arm. It also enables you to look directly down at the ingredient and the knife while cutting, giving you better control over what you are doing.

SLICING

My definition of slicing is to cut something into flat objects; the thinness should range from paper-thin to no greater than ⅛ inch. This method does require some practice, but once the feel of it is acquired, the movement of cutting will come naturally. When one gains control of this basic slicing technique, other methods of cutting will also become easy.

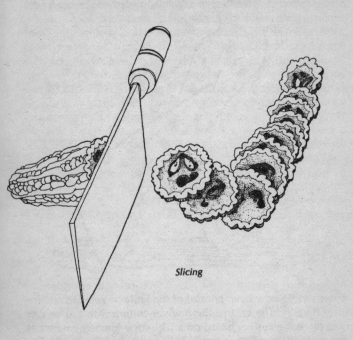

Slicing

Place the item to be sliced on a cutting board. Rest the left hand near one end of this item with the five fingertips close together, forming a line parallel to and near the line where the slice is to be made. The knuckles of the middle fingers form a vertical wall against which the cleaver will slide while all the fingertips are pressing down, out of harm's way. Always hold the left hand in this position while slicing or shredding. With the right hand, grasp the cleaver as described earlier and lay the flat blade against the knuckles of the left hand. These knuckles now act as a stable guide against which the wide blade of the cleaver slides easily and safely. The fingertips of the left hand then work slowly back along the item as the slicing process moves leftward. (Needless to say, left-handed cooks can be expected to change hands in these and later instructions.)

Now start slicing. The best method is to start down the front end of the blade, which is the end farthest away from you. Simultaneously press the knife downward and away from your body. By the time the whole blade has glided through the item a thin slice should be formed. If the piece is still attached to the main part, then you probably did not apply equal pressure all along the cut. The continuing sequence of cutting movements is this: first, the curved fingers move backward a little from the edge of the item; then the knife, which is supported by the knuckles, glides down and forward. When this motion is completed, your fingers should be resting right on the edge of the item again. Remember, the knuckles should always touch the side of the flat blade to serve as a cutting guide. The width of each slice depends solely on how far back the fingers move from the edge.

Parallel Slicing or Splitting

After cutting the ingredient into thin slices, there will sometimes be a thin section left over, the section that is too narrow and too soft to stand upright for straight cutting. In cases like this, lay the piece horizontally on the cutting board and place the palm of the left hand on top of it with the fingers slightly turned upward. With the right hand hold the cleaver parallel to the cutting board and carefully split the item across by sawing with the blade between your palm and the cutting board.

SHREDDING

This method is for cutting ingredients into very thin strips or threadlike slivers. I feel that the word "shred" often confuses people. Those who have not cooked Chinese food probably assume the final appearance of the ingredient should resemble shredded cheese or carrots that have been put through a food processor. But the dictionary's definition for the word "shred" is "a long narrow strip cut or torn off," and that is the exact shape we should try to produce. To achieve the correct form of shred-cutting, first follow the method given for slicing and cut the item into thin slices. Then pile five to eight slices together and repeat the same method as if you were slicing the item again. The result of this double slicing method will then give you the correct, thin, threadlike strips. The length of the strips depends on that of the slices, usually ranging in length from 1 inch to 2½ inches; any strips longer than that should be cut in half. Some people call shred-cutting "julienne-cutting"; I would like to add the word "thin" in front of that, thus defining it as "*thin* julienne-cutting."

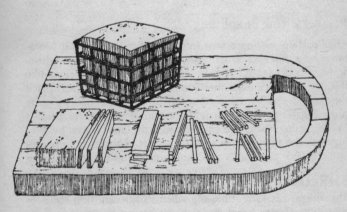

Shredding

MINCING

To Mince Ginger

Scrape the skin off the ginger, slice it into thin pieces, then turn the cleaver upside down and pound the ginger slices with the blunt edge of the knife to break apart the fibers. When the pieces become a pulp, turn the knife over and chop again with the sharp edge until the ginger is finely minced. This method is the best way to mince ginger, since it presses out the juice and breaks the fibers into finer pieces, enabling the flavors and the aroma of ginger to be distributed evenly and to blend in readily with the other ingredients.

To Mince Garlic

Place the clove of garlic on the cutting board and smash it with the flat side of the blade, or place the flat side of the blade on top of the garlic and, with one hand holding the knife, press down with the other hand on top of the blade. This procedure will split open and loosen the skin. Peel and remove the skin. Pound the garlic with the blunt side of the blade until the clove breaks up into small, well-bruised pieces, then reverse the blade and mince until the pieces are very fine.

CHOPPING

There are several different techniques of chopping in Chinese cooking. The one that is applicable for this book is the mincing chop; hence I will omit the other methods and explain only that technique. The size or the fineness provided by the mincing chop is between minced and coarsely chopped. The easy shortcut to obtain these small bits is to first cut the item into thin strips, then hold the strips together in bunches and cut crosswise in as small pieces as possible. Next, push the pieces into a pile and chop until the desired fineness is reached. With leafy vegetables such as spinach and watercress, squeeze the vegetables together into a ball after they have been blanched, and cut randomly into small pieces. Then chop until they become fine bits. For chopping scallions, first split the stalks in two (or quarter them if thick ones are used), then cut crosswise into small pieces and chop.

DICING

The size of a piece of diced ingredient varies from ¼ inch to ½ inch square. If you are cutting everything for a dish from scratch, the size depends entirely on your own preference, but when the dish calls for ingredients such as almonds or peanuts or peas that cannot be cut further, then you must cut the other ingredients to match their size. To dice, start by cutting the ingredients into slices about ⅓ inch thick and then cut each slice into strips ⅓ inch wide. Gather a few strips together and lay them parallel to each other, then cut them crosswise into ⅓-inch squares. If you want some variations in appearance, slant your knife sharply and cut diagonally into diamond-shaped pieces.

ROLL CUTTING

This impressive method is great for cutting firm, cylindrical-shaped vegetables such as asparagus, cucumbers, broccoli, and carrots. Since this type of vegetable is very fibrous and also tightly sealed by a layer of thick skin, it requires a long cooking time if it is not cut properly. The advantage of this technique is that it breaks apart the stringy fibers and exposes as much surface as possible to heat, thus speeding up the cooking while retaining nutritional value.

Place the vegetable on the cutting board, facing from right to left. Start cutting with the knife on one end of the vegetable at an angle ranging from 30 to 45° from the right-left axis. Then roll the vegetable a quarter turn toward yourself and make another similar slice farther up so that the new cut goes into part of the new section and part of the previously cut surface.

Repeat until the whole thing is cut. The different degrees of the slant of your knife determine the exposed surface area of the vegetable. A knife held at a 30° angle will cut a larger area than one held at a 45° angle.

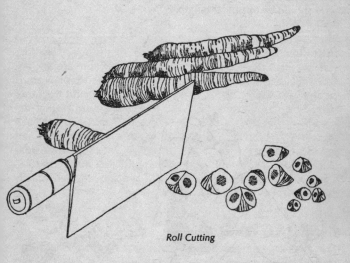

Roll Cutting

CHUNK CUTTING

Of all the cutting methods, this is the easiest one to handle. The basic size of this cut is approximately a 1-inch-square cube. However, instead of cutting every piece into a cube with four neat right angles, the dish will look more attractive if you cut the four sides and four corners unevenly. I call this method wedge cutting. Ingredients such as green peppers look especially inviting when cut in this fashion rather than into a perfect square.

First cut the bulky piece into large strips and follow by cutting the strips randomly into chunks. Though the shape is not extremely important, the dimension of the chunks should still be roughly the same. When cutting semi-flat objects such as green peppers into uneven-sided quadrangles or polygons, the shape of the chunks may not be uniform, but their perimeter should be of similar length.

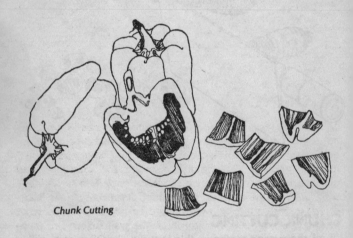

Chunk Cutting

COOKING METHODS

There are at least twenty-six Chinese characters used for cooking terms. Each one designates a special method of preparing the food. These terms appear widely in Chinese restaurant menus to indicate how the dish is cooked and with what kind of ingredients. An experienced Chinese cook knows perfectly well just what he must do to the food according to the characters, and a connoisseur of Chinese cuisine also knows what to expect when he gives his order to the waiter. Many of these terms apply to preparing meat only; some are used exclusively among professional cooks, ordinary simple home meals seldom needing to be cooked in such an elaborate fashion. Here I give a few of the basic cooking methods that are most commonly practiced in making Chinese dishes, methods that will be used repeatedly throughout this book. With the help of this section you will get a better understanding of the basics of Chinese cooking.

STIR-FRYING

Stir-frying is the best-known cooking technique developed by the Chinese. It is a very efficient way of solving the problem of the scarcity of fuel while retaining flavor and nutrition. In stir-frying the materials are first cut into small pieces of various shapes, depending on the nature of the dish; however, all the components that go into the same dish must be cut uniformly to conform to the principal ingredient of the dish. For example, if you are preparing a dish in which noodles are the major ingredient, anything that is going to be added to the dish has to be cut into thin strips to match the shape of the noodles. Next, the ingredients are cooked with a small amount of oil in a wok over very intense heat for at most a few minutes— and sometimes 10 seconds or less. During the actual period of cooking the ingredients are tossed, stirred, and turned over constantly in order to move the raw pieces on top down to the bottom to be cooked and the bottom ones to the top. This technique is similar to the Western method of sautéeing, but the Chinese carry it one step further by cooking the sautéed food again with steam. That is, after the sautéeing step, if the items still require more cooking, a small amount of liquid is added. Then the pan is covered tightly for a couple of minutes to allow the steam generated from the vigorous boiling of the liquid to accelerate the cooking process.

This method is particularly good for cooking vegetables. The high temperatures help bring out the original flavor of the vegetables, seal in the juices, intensify their natural color, preserve their basic texture, and retain food nutrients. One important trick to remember is to remove vegetables from the fire slightly *under*cooked; the residual heat will continue to cook them, and by the time the dish reaches the table it will be just right. However, if you like your vegetables a bit well done, by all means leave them in the pan until the degree of doneness reaches your preference. The result will be just as delicious. Either way, the taste is still far superior to boiled vegetables, which by contrast are very dull and insipid.

A Few Guidelines for Stir-Frying

In stir-frying the cooking time is extremely short. After the cooking has started, it cannot be interrupted; it is impossible to stop in the midst of tossing and stirring to prepare an overlooked item. Therefore it is important to get all the preparation done in advance:

1. Double-check the recipe to see if all the ingredients are cut according to the instructions.
2. Be sure that vegetables are washed and properly cut to the shape and size designated by the recipe.
3. See that washed vegetables are drained thoroughly; shake off as much water as possible. Excess water will reduce the temperature of the oil and adversely affect the cooking process. Also, when water is mixed with hot oil it causes the oil to splatter furiously and can burn your hands and face.
4. If a cornstarch solution is called for in the recipe, mix it in advance. All the ingredients should be placed within easy reach of the stove. You may want to put each item in a separate bowl and arrange the ingredients in the order they are to be put into the pan. To minimize your work, if the seasoning ingredients are all to be added at the same time, you can combine them in a small bowl or a cup beforehand. Thus, when it is time to flavor the food, all you have to do is pour the mixture into the pan rather than adding the seasonings one at a time.
5. When cooking vegetables, the heat should be kept at the maximum high temperature throughout the entire cooking time. Vegetables that generate their own juice, such as spinach and bean sprouts, should be cooked in less time. When cooking firmer vegetables like broccoli and cauliflower, which do not produce any juice, a small amount of stock or water should be added to provide steam and to cook the vegetables more evenly. When vegetables are being cooked covered, it is best not to lift the lid since the vegetables will become dull and yellowish if you do.

Given the above preliminary cautions, set the wok over a

high flame and heat for about a minute, or until a few drops of water sprinkled into the wok jump around vigorously, indicating that the pan is ready for cooking. The time required to heat up the wok or pan will of course vary, depending on what kind of metal the utensil is made of and how thick it is. Next, add oil and swirl it around to coat the pan. The heat of the pan will warm up the oil immediately and it should flow smoothly. Now, quickly drop in the ingredients and then add the seasonings. Meanwhile, with one hand holding the handle of the wok and the other hand holding the spatula, keep stirring and tossing the ingredients. The order in which ingredients are added should precisely follow the instructions in each recipe. Aromatic seasonings such as garlic, ginger root, scallion, etc., are generally added to the hot oil before the other ingredients, so that their flavors will permeate the rest of the dish. The cornstarch solution is always added near the end of cooking and should be stirred gradually into the hot liquid until the sauce is thickened and smooth. Then stir and coat ingredients evenly with the thickened sauce.

While stir-frying food one must be as alert as possible. There is no dogmatic rule that will guarantee a perfect result. The Chinese believe that while you are engaged in stir-frying, your five senses should be at their top receptivity. The eyes should keep close watch on the food as it changes in color and texture; the ears should detect every cracking and sizzling sound that signals the stage of doneness of the food; the nose checks whether the ingredients are releasing the proper aroma; the mouth tastes the flavor of the seasonings; and above all, your body and soul should feel harmony with the action.

Precise, step-by-step cooking instructions are given in every recipe in this book; they should be followed exactly. The procedures of the stir-fried dishes may seem more or less alike, but, because the ingredients used in each dish differ, the cutting, sequence of use, and timing will differ. Dishes such as Stir-Fried Spinach (page 185) will be cooked in a much shorter time and with no need for the steaming process, while Stir-Fried Broccoli (page 184) will require slightly longer cooking time and must be covered and steamed with some liquid.

A Word about Oil

Vegetable oils such as cottonseed oil, peanut oil, corn oil, safflower oil, etc., are all perfect for stir-frying. Personally, I prefer good corn oil to any other kind of oil. Other vegetable oils, when heated, give off a certain odor. I have a very sensitive nose, and when I cook with these oils I immediately develop a headache. Good corn oil, however, seems to remain odorless no matter how hot it gets. Butter should never be used for stir-frying nor for deep frying; it burns too easily. Since dairy products have never been common to the Chinese diet, foods cooked with butter cannot taste authentically Chinese. And, of course, butter is totally inappropriate in pure vegetarian cooking.

Woks

The best pan for stir-frying food is the Chinese wok. A wok is a wide, round pan with a curved bottom. "Can Chinese food be cooked without a wok?" This is a question frequently asked by my students; the answer is "Of course." One can always put an elaborate Chinese meal together with limited cooking equipment. Where there is a will there is a way. As a matter of fact, a modern American kitchen equipped with the latest cooking utensils is more than adequate for cooking things Chinese. A heavy dutch oven, a high-rim cast-iron skillet, and a thick saucepan are all reasonably good cooking implements for preparing Chinese dishes.

Although the wok is not absolutely essential then, it is a wonderful thing to add to the kitchen. One wok is equal to many pots and pans. A wok can be used to stir-fry, deep-fry, boil, braise, steam, smoke, pan-fry, simmer, and stew; sometimes at the end of cooking their meal the Chinese even use it as a basin for washing the dishes. In addition, its rounded bottom provided a perfect fit for the old-style Chinese burners, which used a variety of fuels such as wood, straw, twigs, and dried dung. The shape also made it possible for one wok to serve the function of several other kinds of implements, because you can cook any amount of food in the same wok simply by adjusting the fire. The curved bottom is ideal for stir-frying since it requires very little oil for cooking; thus the food does not turn out greasy. The surrounding high rim also serves as a shield to prevent oil from splattering all over, and at the same time it provides the maximum area for stirring food. In recent years all sorts of metals have been used to make woks, but the traditional ones are made of iron, since iron conducts heat more evenly. Stainless steel is a very poor conductor of heat. If you are buying only one, a 14-inch wok is the perfect size for family use. A small-sized one is very cute but not practical; even so, it might be nice to have one in the kitchen as a second wok for special uses, such as deep-frying to save oil. Electric woks are handsome, but the heating element on the bottom is too small and does not generate enough heat to do most serious cooking. However, they can be useful for handling small portions of food or for deep-frying.

When a new wok is bought it must be treated before being used; the process is called "seasoning the wok." Scrub the entire inside of the wok with cleansing powder as if you were cleaning your sink, then rinse it thoroughly and dry with paper towels. Set the wok on the stove, pour in ⅓ cup of vegetable oil, and heat over a low flame for 15 minutes. Tilt the pan from side to side and swirl the oil around in the wok constantly, making sure the oil coats the entire surface. Discard the oil and wipe off the remainder with paper towels. The wok is now ready for use. Repeated use will improve the seasoning. Wash your wok with hot soapy water and dry thoroughly after each use.

Cover, Spatula, Ring Stand

To go along with the wok you will need an aluminum cover and a metal spatula. The diameter of the cover usually is a few inches shorter than the diameter of the wok, so that it fits neatly about 2 inches below the edge of the rim. A spatula with a stainless-steel shovel-like blade and a handle of wood or plastic is ideal. A pancake turner will work perfectly well.

In order to get maximum heat when I stir-fry food, I set my wok directly on top of the stove without using a ring stand. However, because of the rounded bottom, the wok tends to rock around quite a bit, so for those who are novices at using a wok, I recommend a ring stand to support the wok, particularly if you are deep-frying.

Those who cook on an electric stove should try to do without the ring stand as soon as they have gained some experience. The heat coming from an electric stove usually is not intense enough to stir-fry a large amount of food, but setting the wok directly on top of the heating element will compensate somewhat. Remember to keep the heat at the highest setting at all times throughout the cooking process. If the wok gets too hot in the midst of your cooking just remove it from the element for a few seconds to cool, then return it to the high heat. Since electric elements take quite a while to heat and cool, and since the stir-frying process cannot be interrupted, it is much more effective to move the wok to one side rather than to wait for the heating elements to get hot or cold.

STEAMING

In steam cooking food is cooked by the force of steam generated from rapidly boiling water. Steaming is another widely practiced, favorite way of cooking among the Chinese because it is easy and does not require constant watching. When I was a child, there were always two steamed dishes at every meal in our family, in addition to a soup and a couple of stir-fried dishes. The reason steamed items are served so regularly is because most of the time in Chinese home cooking the heat generated from steaming rice is utilized to cook one or two other dishes, which are prepared in the same pot simultaneously, saving both time and fuel. Thus, with proper planning and sequencing, one burner is sufficient to prepare a meal composed of several separate dishes. Generally the rice has to be cooked in advance of other dishes and must be set aside for about 15 minutes before serving. Foods that are steamed in the same pot with the rice will stay warm during this period, and meanwhile the burner is free for preparing other dishes. The food to be steamed is placed in a heat-proof plate or bowl and supported over the rice on a rack. Since steaming retains the maximum natural flavor of the ingredients, the most delicate foods are cooked using this method, which brings out their best features and also preserves their good taste.

There are two ways of steaming. In one method the ingredients are placed in a shallow dish; the dish is then set in a pot, supported by a rack, with the dish uncovered but the pot tightly closed. The food is cooked by direct contact with the steam generated from the boiling water. Dishes such as the Steamed Eggs with Scallion (page 222) and Steamed Fresh Eggs with Salted Eggs (page 223) are cooked this way.

In the other form of steaming, the ingredients are put into a deep earthenware container covered with a lid, which is then placed either on a rack or directly inside a large pan with 2 inches of water. The large pan is then covered and the food in the container is cooked by the surrounding boiling water. Mushroom Soup (page 96) is prepared in this manner. The main purpose of this kind of cooking is to extract the original flavor of the ingredients and dissolve their essence into the broth.

There are utensils that are especially made for steaming, some of bamboo and some of aluminum. The bamboo ones look like baskets and are very decorative. They come in several tiers, one set on top of the other and then covered with a bamboo lid which comes with the set. When you are steaming food that is to be cooked directly in the serving dish, the dish can be placed right on the bare bamboo of the basket. With such things as steamed buns and dumplings, the tiers should be lined with a few large vegetable leaves or with a piece of damp cheesecloth or perforated aluminum foil. One of the disadvantages of bamboo steamers is they have to be set on top of a wok or some other large pan. If you only own one wok, the constant use of boiling water will damage the smooth coat of seasoning. Aluminum steamers are quite handy to have; a set usually comes with two tiers plus a bottom pot for water and a cover. The bottom of each tier is perforated to allow the easy flow of hot steam.

But one can still cook all the fancy dishes without a set of steamers. You can improvise with what is available in the kitchen. All you need are a good-sized dutch oven, or a wok, or a deep pot that has a lid, and a cake rack or a ring 1½ inches high made by removing both ends of a tin can. The rack is for supporting the plate of food to keep it away from the water. The bottom of the plate should be about 2 inches above the level of the water, so that when the water is boiling it will not splash into the plate. There also should be an inch of space between the plate and the edges of the pan to allow the steam to circulate. The water in the pot should be boiling vigorously at all times throughout the steaming period to generate enough steam to cook the food. During this time the pot should be covered tightly and should be uncovered as seldom as possible. For prolonged steaming, the boiling water must be replenished from time to time. After cooking is completed, turn off the heat, stand a little back from the pot, and lift up the cover carefully. Allow the steam to disperse before removing the food. To avoid burning your hands, wear a pair of rubber gloves while lifting the dish from the pan.

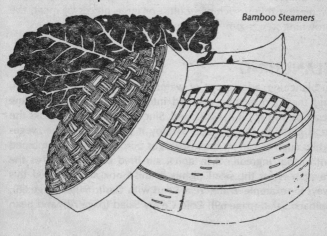

Bamboo Steamers

BRAISING

Braising is actually two cooking steps combined in one. The technique of Chinese braising is much the same as fricasseeing in Western cooking. First the ingredients are browned in hot oil to sear them slightly and seal in the juices; next, a small amount of liquid is added and the ingredients are simmered covered or uncovered for a few minutes. The browning process adds extra flavor to the foods and also dehydrates them a little; thus, when a tasty sauce is added, it is absorbed quickly and blended into the foods to enhance the flavor. To cook chicken, fish, and tofu in this way brings out the best of their natural taste and original texture. In this book Braised Tofu (page 126), Braised Deep-Fried Tofu Puffs (page 124), Braised Eggplant (page 175), and Braised Chinese Radish (page 194) are cooked with this method. A wok or a heavy skillet is suitable for braising. With the exception of braised fish, braised dishes generally can be prepared ahead of time and reheated just before serving. When the preliminary braising steps are followed, and more broth and soy sauce and other seasonings are added to the ingredients, which are then simmered covered for a longer period of time, the Chinese call it red-simmering or red-stewing. In red-simmering things such as poultry or large pieces of meat, the browning step is sometimes omitted.

BLANCHING

In blanching, a large pot of water is brought to a rolling boil, and the food is then plunged into the water for just a few seconds, or until it has softened. Since this technique cooks the food partially, the Chinese employ it to soften tougher vegetables such as carrots and asparagus before they are combined with other ingredients in quick stir-fried dishes. Most of the vegetables for the salad dishes in this book are prepared this way, for example Watercress Salad with Garlic Salad (page 66), Spinach Salad (page 69), Cold Celery Salad (page 72), and Bean

Sprout and Egg Thread Salad (page 74), which are all marvelous dishes, simple to make and delicious. The Chinese rarely eat their vegetables raw, for sanitary reasons; the blanching process kills off parasites. The length of time needed to blanch food varies from ingredient to ingredient. Soft vegetables like spinach and bean sprouts need only a few seconds; firm vegetables such as cabbage and carrots usually require longer time.

DEEP-FRYING

The Chinese method of deep-frying is more or less similar to the Western one: foods are dropped into a large quantity of hot oil and cooked until done. Deep-frying is used more frequently to cook meat than vegetables. In cooking meat, the Chinese quite often deep-fry the food in two stages. The first step hardens the surface and seals in the juice; in the second step the oil is heated until it is very hot and the ingredients are returned to the oil and fried until golden brown. To deep-fry vegetables one step is sufficient. This frying step tenderizes the vegetables and also brings out their delicate flavors. The string beans in String Beans Szechuan-Style (page 172) and String Beans Stir-Fried with Bamboo Shoots and Mushrooms (page 171) and the eggplant in Spicy Eggplant (page 176) would taste very bland if the deep-frying step were omitted. To deep-fry foods that are easily cooked, the oil should be very hot. The hotter the oil the quicker the outside layer of food forms a hard crust and becomes less absorbent; hence, the food is less greasy. On the other hand, when deep-frying nuts, such as the walnuts in Mock Sweet and Sour Pork (page 155), the oil cannot be so hot that it burns the ingredients.

Again, a wok is a perfect utensil for deep-frying; otherwise a deep fryer or any deep pot will do. I like to use a cast-iron skillet to deep-fry egg rolls, because large amounts of oil are not required; 1 inch of oil is usually enough. Moreover the skillet can accommodate more rolls per batch than a wok and it is easier to put them in and take them out.

SIMMERING

Simmering must be the most common cooking method throughout the world; it is used to prepare both soups and stews. In this method food is cooked with liquid in a heavy kettle over low heat for a considerable length of time. It is one of the best ways to prepare foods that need prolonged cooking. The food and liquid are first brought to a boil over high heat, which is then reduced so that there is only enough heat to generate small bubbles on the surface. Unlike boiling, in which the liquid rolls very vigorously over high heat and evaporates very rapidly, simmering retains most of the broth in the pot; the slow cooking extracts the goodness of the ingredients into the broth, making it rich in taste. A rich stock such as Soybean Sprout Stock (page 90) should be simmered for a long time. Heavy kettles or electric crock pots are most suitable for simmering food.

TOASTING

There are a few ingredients in this book that require dry toasting. The method is used to prepare the sesame seeds for the dessert dish Sesame Slices (page 282) and the Szechuan peppercorns for Spicy Bean Curd (page 127). Toasting means to cook dry ingredients in an un-oiled pan over a low flame until they become brown; stir and toss them constantly while they are being toasted. This method brings out the aroma of the materials and at the same time dries them. A cast-iron skillet is best for toasting.

HOW TO
PLAN A CHINESE
VEGETARIAN MEAL

*A daily meal should not be extravagant,
but the dinner for guests certainly
ought to be luxurious.*

—Chinese folk saying

A Chinese vegetarian meal generally is not the kind of feast that impresses guests with its rich and rare ingredients, but rather lets the diners discover by themselves the wonderfully delicate tastes that are hidden in all those plebeian foods. So the flavor of each dish should be carefully chosen—sharp contrasting with mild, a strongly seasoned dish with a light, subtle one. Present each dish with equal emphasis and give each its true identity. Equally important in a Chinese meal is the variety in texture; thus, remember that something crunchy goes with something creamy, and something crispy with something soft. Though each of the dishes is entirely different in character, when served together they should complement each other in a lively unity. The visual effect should be another important consideration; the food presented at the table should be pleasing to the eye and inviting to the senses. Whether you are arranging mock duck on a plate or placing broccoli in a bowl, try to employ some of your artistic talents.

Designing a vegetarian meal undoubtedly requires a bit more thinking and planning, and it probably demands extra effort from those who are not familiar with Chinese cooking. But have no fear; once you acquire a few basic methods for cooking one Chinese dish, the rest will come easily and soon you will be cooking a whole meal as if you had been doing it all your life.

If this is your first venture into Chinese cooking, try a dish at a time (and perhaps the same dish several times) at the beginning. You will very quickly become an expert on those dishes and at the same time gain a solid repertoire. When cooking for company or planning a three-course meal, there should be one cold dish, which can be prepared in advance and arranged on a plate waiting to be served. Another dish might be a stew or a braised dish that need only be reheated, leaving just one dish for last-minute stir-frying. Regardless of the number of courses in a dinner, if only one person is doing the cooking there should not be more than two last-minute stir-fried dishes, and these two should be separated by other dishes in the serving sequence. For those who need a guide in selecting dishes for a meal, I have prepared some sample menus (pages 37–39). This list will help to get you started; you can then branch out and create more combinations on your own. The possibilities are unlimited.

FAMILY-STYLE VS. BANQUET-STYLE MEALS

A Chinese family meal, serving four to six people, usually consists of four to five dishes plus rice. At each meal there are meat dishes, a fish dish, a vegetable dish, and a simple soup. The meat dishes are usually made up of a small amount of pork or beef cut and stir-fried with seasonal vegetables; the fish dish is prepared from whatever seafood is available; the soup is light soup, with ingredients that can be combined with water and cooked in just a few minutes. Sometimes there is a very salty dish, such as steamed salted fish or spicy pickles, which serves as a standby when the diners are especially hungry and need something more to accompany an extra bowl of rice. When dining with family, the dishes are served simultaneously; there is no particular sequence as to what should be put on the table first. Soup, for instance, is served at the same time as all the other dishes; the diners help themselves to some soup in a small bowl or drink a spoonful at a time directly from the main soup tureen. An informal dinner with close friends is also served in this fashion.

For banquets, the Chinese switch to a more Western, formal dining style, that is, one course at a time. However, there are many more courses in a Chinese banquet than in a Western formal dinner. A Chinese banquet is divided into sets, and each set has several courses. In the old days an elaborate banquet ranged from thirty-six to forty-six courses; today banquets range from fourteen to twenty-one courses. This figure is based on the traditional dining habits outside of the People's Republic of China.

MENUS

Here are suggestions for two-course meals for informal weekend lunches, quick suppers, or late-evening snacks, and for three-course and four-course dinners. In this book each dish, if served with rice, is generally sufficient for two or three people; the exceptions are the noodle dishes, which, without rice, can serve as light meals for three or four people.

LIGHT MEALS FOR TWO TO FOUR

Menu 1
   Scallion Pancakes
   Deep-Fried Bean Curd and Mung Bean Noodle Soup
Menu 2
   Spring Rolls (egg rolls)
   Hot and Sour Soup
Menu 3
   Szechuan Spicy Noodles
   Bean Sprout and
   Egg-Thread Salad

Menu 4
  Fried Dumplings and Steamed Dumplings
  Spinach Egg-Drop Soup

Dinner Menus for Four to Six

Menu 1
  Braised Bean Curd
  Tomato Egg-Drop Soup
  Braised Mung Bean Noodles
  Rice and tea

Menu 2
  Green Peppers with Mock Meat (stir-fried green peppers
    with pressed bean curd)
  Braised Eggplant
  Five-Spice Eggs
  Rice and tea

Menu 3
  Mock Roast Duck
  Goddess of Mercy Soup (bean curd soup with tiger lily
    buds and tree ears)
  Chinese Mustard Greens in Black Bean Sauce
  Rice and tea

Menu 4
  Cauliflower and Bean Curd Sticks
  Mixed Pressed Bean Curd Threads
  Soybean Soup with Fried Gluten
  Rice and tea

Menu 5
  Spinach Salad
  Szechuan Spicy Noodles
  Spicy Bean Sprout Rolls
  Tea

Menu 6
  Two-Sides-Brown Noodles
  Seaweed and Bean Curd Soup
  Bean Sprout and Egg-Thread Salad
  Tea

Dinner Menus for Six to Eight

Menu 1
  Mock Moo Goo Gai Pan
  Bean Curd with Oyster Sauce
  Braised Bamboo Shoots with Pickled Mustard Greens
  Velvet Corn Soup
  Rice and tea
Menu 2
  Pressed Bean Curd Salad
  Asparagus with Three Kinds of Mushrooms
  Fried Mock Squab
  Braised Chinese Radish
  Rice and tea
Menu 3
  Lo-Han Vegetable Dish
  Mock Ham
  Spinach Salad
  Spicy Bean Curd
  Rice and tea
Menu 4
  Mock Abalone
  Deep-Fried Bean Curd and Mung Bean Noodle Soup
  Mock Spicy Chicken
  Steamed Vegetable Rice
  Tea

INGREDIENTS

*Mild flavor is superior to strong taste and
vulgarity is inferior to refinement.*

—Talks on Roots and Vegetables,
by Hung Tzu-ch'eng (Ming Dynasty)

Good ingredients and proper seasonings are of the utmost
importance for all successful Chinese dishes. Soy sauce is not
used in every Chinese dish, nor is it added to the food randomly. The sweet, pure, subtle flavor of chicken broth is im-
paired by adding soy sauce; yet a braised fish without soy sauce
is dull-tasting. To a Chinese cook there is a set pattern in
blending the correct seasonings together into each dish. Every
grain of salt and every drop of soy sauce that go into a certain
dish should be in harmony with the nature of the rest of the
ingredients; the flavors should complement each other and
never clash.

There are differences in the use of seasonings and spices that
serve to distinguish the various regional cuisines, even though
the basic ingredients are largely the same across China. For
instance, Cantonese cooking is subtle: it emphasizes the natural
flavors of the ingredients and thus never mixes dark soy sauce
in a dish for which only light soy sauce is appropriate, or vice
versa. Szechuan cuisine is noted for spicy hot dishes such as
Spicy Eggplant (page 176) and Spicy Bean Curd (page 127).
Shanghai cooking tends to lean a bit heavily on sugar and soy
sauce; dishes like Mock Lion's Head (page 138), Spinach Salad
(page 69), and Mixed Cold Noodles (page 257) are famous
Shanghai dishes. The north, around Peking and the Shantung

area, is the cradle of Chinese court dishes. However, the use of mutton in this cuisine reflects the influence of their neighbor Mongolia. Fukien is known for rich soups made from seafood gathered from its rivers and ocean; Fukien's shredded pork and shredded fish dishes are also famous throughout China.

In vegetarian cooking, however, the distinction between regions is less clear. There were, and may still be, good vegetarian restaurants in Shanghai which serve food similar to that served in vegetarian restaurants in Hong Kong and Taiwan.

A Word about MSG

MSG—monosodium glutamate or Accent—is a chemical from natural sources that is used to bolster the flavor of many foods. Nowadays some cooks and restaurant chefs tend to add a touch of MSG to everything they prepare. I heartily disapprove! The indiscriminate use of this chemical is at best an admission of lack of confidence in oneself and one's ingredients; at worst it can generate bad side effects of a yet unstudied nature. The so-called Chinese Restaurant Syndrome refers to the dizziness and even fainting spells that have been caused by over-use of MSG. You will find no MSG called for in my entire book. I advocate enhancing flavors solely by means of careful blending of the best ingredients available.

BASICS TO KEEP ON HAND

I have never seen anything spread as speedily as has the use of Chinese ingredients and cooking utensils in recent years. The growing popularity of Chinese food in America and Europe is indeed amazing. This ancient cuisine is charging into every Western kitchen in full force. As I recall, just a decade ago in America one could hardly find a small section of ginger root on sale anywhere except in "Chinatowns" or small neighborhood Oriental groceries. Today tofu, bamboo shoots, fresh bean sprouts, snow peas, bok choy, giant icicle radishes, wonton wrappers, Szechuan peppercorns, dried tree ears fungi, and other ingredients have become common staples in supermarkets throughout the nation, especially in places where there is an Oriental community. For those who are inspired by this exotic cuisine and would like to add Chinese culinary skills to their cooking repertoire, I suggest stocking a cupboard with a few essential ingredients. If you live in an area where Oriental ingredients are not easily obtained, having the basics on hand will eliminate a great deal of last-minute hustle, particularly if you intend to try a few dishes at regular intervals. Many of the seasoning agents are quite inexpensive, so stock up on as many varieties as you think you might need. Most of the canned foods will keep indefinitely if stored in a dry, cool place. Fresh tofu will keep from two to three weeks in the refrigerator if it is soaked in water that is changed every day. Fried bean curd puffs and fried wheat gluten can be frozen indefinitely. All the dried products made from soybean milk, which are high-protein substances, should be kept in dry, cool place to prevent them from becoming rancid. Canned pickled items will keep for a long time after opening if they are transferred to jars and kept in the refrigerator. Fresh Chinese vegetables might present a problem. However, some things such as fresh bean sprouts can easily be raised right in your hall closet (see page 163 on how to grow bean sprouts). Such typical ingredients for Chinese cooking as string beans, broccoli, spinach, and eggplant are readily available. Other ingredients such as mustard greens and snow peas will grow beautifully in your backyard garden during the summer months. Bamboo shoots, water chestnuts, and litchees are all preserved very nicely in cans and are widely available in supermarkets.

Here is a list of some commonly used seasonings. A more detailed glossary follows this list.

Brown bean paste or brown bean sauce
    Comes in cans. Once it is opened, transfer to a jar and it will keep indefinitely in the refrigerator.
Fermented white bean curd (tofu-ru)
    Comes in jars. Just put the jar into the refrigerator and it will still be good after seven years.

Fermented black beans
Store in a jar and keep in the refrigerator. They might get dry after six months, but will still be good.

Chili oil
If kept in cool place, it will last indefinitely.

Cornstarch

Ginger root
Store in the vegetable drawer in the refrigerator without wrapping and it will keep for one to two months.

Garlic
Keep in the pantry or the refrigerator.

Hoisin sauce
Will keep for a long time in the refrigerator in a glass container.

Oil
I prefer corn oil, but any vegetable oil will do.

Oyster sauce
Expensive but lasts a long time. Must be kept in the refrigerator.

Rice wine or Chinese Shao-sing wine
Japanese sake, dry sherry, or even gin can substitute. Store the rice wine in a cool place or in the refrigerator.

Scallions
Keep a couple of bunches in the refrigerator at all times.

Sesame oil
Will stay good for a long time, even without refrigeration.

Soy sauce
For all-purpose cooking. Japanese soy sauce from the supermarket will do.

Szechuan hot bean paste
Will keep indefinitely in the refrigerator after transferring from can to a jar.

Szechuan peppercorns
Store in a plastic bag or a sealed container and they will keep indefinitely.

Stock
Keep a few vegetarian bouillon cubes on hand or make a large quantity of vegetarian stock according to the recipe on

pages 90–91. Then freeze in separate small containers (yogurt cartons are useful). For detailed information, see page 62 on "Stock."

GLOSSARY

The following glossary lists only those items that need to be explained; familiar ingredients are not listed.

Agar Agar
Dried white gum made from seaweed. Comes in two different forms; one is in sticks about an inch thick and the other is in thin, noodle-like strips. Both types are about 12 inches long. The thick ones are melted in boiling water and used as unflavored gelatin; the thin ones are soaked in cold water and added to cold vegetable dishes.

Baby Corn on the Cob
A relatively new ingredient to this country, but rapidly gaining popularity. Used to stir-fry with other vegetables, it is actually a miniature variety of corn on the cob; it is very tender, and the whole ear is edible. Each ear is about two inches long; if larger

ones are used, they should be cut in two, lengthwise. Available in cans at Chinese grocery stores or the gourmet section of some larger supermarkets.

Bamboo Shoots
In China there are many varieties of bamboo shoots and they grow at different times of the year. Some bamboo shoots are named after the four seasons, according to the time they are available. For instance, winter bamboo shoots are gathered at the end of winter before the young shoots become full grown. They are the tastiest of all bamboo shoots. Spring bamboo shoots are harvested in the spring; the shoots are very large, and most of the canned bamboo shoots are of this species. Canned bamboo shoots are obtainable in the United States. Once opened, they should be covered with water and stored in the refrigerator. Change the water three times a week and they will keep for a couple of months.

Bean Curd (See page 119.)

Bean Curd, Deep-Fried Puffs (See page 120.)

Bean Curd, Fermented Red (Nan-Ru)
Many cookbooks give the wrong definition for this ingredient. Because the Chinese name for this is "nan-ru," meaning "southern fermented bean curd," many people assume that it is made out of bean curd. However this special ingredient has nothing to do with soybeans or bean curd; instead it is made of taro root. Taro root is first steamed until tender, then mashed and blended with flour and salt and left in an earthen container for two weeks until it is covered with mold. It is then dried in the sun and formed into square pieces and covered with a mixture of wine, soy sauce, and saltpeter. After being aged for a couple of months it is ready for use. Very tasty when cooked with vegetables; it enhances their flavor.

Bean Curd, Fermented White (Tofu-Ru)
Tofu-ru is somewhat like blue cheese, in that you either love it at first taste or you need a considerable length of time to appreciate its distinctive flavor. Though fermented bean curd does

not have the same strong smell as blue cheese, its taste is equally sharp. The consistency of well-ripened tofu-ru is very soft and creamy; when put into the mouth it melts instantly.

Tofu-ru is fermented by leaving a firmer type of bean curd in a warm place (about 90°) for four to six days until the bean curd is covered with about ½ inch of mold. The fermented bean curd is then soaked in brine mixed with rice wine and spices. After aging for a couple of months, it is ready for use.

Tofu-ru sold in the United States usually comes in a jar; the pieces are about an inch square and are beige in color. There are plain and spiced varieties, and both will keep indefinitely in the refrigerator. Fermented bean curd can be added to all stir-fried vegetables; since it is quite salty, the amount of salt or soy sauce in the recipe should be reduced.

Bean Curd, Five-Spice Pressed (See page 123.)

Bean Curd, Plain Pressed (See page 122.)

Bean Curd, Pressed Bean Curd Threads or Pressed Bean Curd Noodles
This ingredient looks almost exactly like noodles but is made from bean curd. The threads are made by pressing a large cake of bean curd under a hand-turned screw press until most of the water has been removed, then running it through a noodle-making machine that cuts it into thin strips. Pressed bean curd noodles have a chewy, meaty texture. They are excellent in soups or in salads blended with vegetables and are available in bean curd shops or Chinese grocery stores; they can also be made at home with the recipe in this book (page 122) by cutting unflavored pressed bean curd cakes into thin strips.

Bean Curd Sheets (Tofu-pi)
Bean curd sheets are also known as bean curd skins and bean curd robes. The difficulty in giving a proper translation from Chinese to English for this ingredient is probably related to the fact that bean curd sheets are not true bean curd in the strictest sense, because they do not undergo the same chemical co-agulating process as does bean curd. They are made directly by

heating soy milk over a very slow flame for about 10 minutes until a thin film is formed on the surface. This layer of soy milk sheet then is lifted up and drained. It is somewhat similar to the film of cream that forms on top of milk after it has been heated.

Bean curd sheets are somewhat unknown in the West, but they are as widely used in Chinese cooking as regular bean curd and are one of the most essential ingredients in Chinese Buddhist cuisine. There are several forms of bean curd sheets. Some come in circular shapes and some in rectangles; there are fresh and dried varieties, and there are differences in thickness as well. The type that is generally available in the States is the dried one, but if you live in a city that has a Chinatown, most of the Chinese grocery stores there will carry fresh bean curd sheets as well as dried ones.

Bean Curd Sheets, Er-Ju

Er-ju bean curd sheets are a thicker form of bean curd sheet made from the settled sediment of soybean milk. They are prepared by folding the bean curd sheet into two or three layers and then cutting into pieces 1½ inches wide by 5 inches long. Sheets are sold dried, tied up like a stack of cards, and should be soaked in water for 15 minutes before being used.

Bean Curd Sheets, Pressed or Hundred-Leaf (Bai-Yeh)

Do not confuse pressed bean curd sheets with dried or fresh bean curd sheets, which are made from soy milk. Pressed bean curd sheets are made from the actual bean curd. The Mandarin name for pressed bean curd sheets is "bai-yeh," meaning "one hundred leaves"; the Cantonese call it "one hundred sheets." It is so named because this unique type of bean curd is made by pouring a thin layer of bean curd onto a piece of cloth and then piling many sheets of cloth and curd on top of one another; these are then pressed together until the bean curd becomes dry and pliable. The cloth is then peeled off, leaving a thin sheet of dried bean curd that looks like a thin piece of cloth. Pressed bean curd sheets generally come in an 8-inch square sheet that has a clothlike pattern imprinted on it. It is much softer in texture than bean curd sheets.

Bai-yeh is used for making mock chicken; it is also cut into strips and stir-fried with vegetables. Sometimes bai-yeh is first rolled up and then tied into knots for braised dishes or soups. It can be purchased from Chinese grocery stores either fresh or frozen.

Bean Curd Sticks

Bean curd sticks are made the same way as bean curd sheets, except bean curd sticks have been folded. They are interchangeable in stir-fried dishes with bean curd sheets.

Brown Bean Paste, or Brown Bean Sauce

Made from soybeans and salt with flour added to serve as a fermenting agent. It is quite salty, but when a small amount is blended with vegetables or meat it enhances the flavor of the dish. Brown bean paste comes in two forms, one with the beans still whole, the other with beans ground up into a smooth paste. They are interchangeable as far as taste is concerned, except that the ground form blends in more evenly with delicate ingredients. Brown bean paste is sold in cans and in jars. Once the can is opened, the paste should be transferred to a jar and stored in the refrigerator. Available in Oriental grocery stores. Japanese soybean miso can be substituted.

Bean Paste, Szechuan Hot Bean or Spicy Soy

Made the same way and contains the same ingredients as brown bean paste, but with spicy chili added. It not only has all the subtle flavors of the brown bean sauce but has the extra zest of peppery chili. Hot bean paste comes in cans; once opened, paste should be transferred to a jar and kept in the refrigerator.

Bean Sprouts, Mung

The sprouts of mung beans are milky white shoots with olive-green tops. They can be eaten raw, but the Chinese prefer to stir-fry them with meat and other vegetables or to blanch them in boiling water for a few seconds and serve them cold as salad. Available fresh in Chinese grocery stores or large supermarkets, they can also be grown at home with the instructions given in this book. Mung bean sprouts are also available in cans but are not a good substitute for fresh.

Bean Sprouts, Soy or Yellow

This variety of bean sprouts is grown from soybeans. The size of these sprouts is larger than mung bean sprouts; the texture is not as crisp, but the flavor is much more tasty. They also require longer cooking time. Available in Chinese grocery stores and large supermarkets, they can also be sprouted at home with instructions given in this book. For best results, new-crop soybeans should be used. Soybean sprouts should be kept in a closed plastic bag and stored in the refrigerator.

Bok Choy

The most commonly used Chinese green vegetable. Bok choy somewhat resembles Swiss chard, only the stems are whiter and the leaves are darker. Sold fresh by the bunch in Chinese grocery stores or in the Oriental section of some supermarkets.

Chili Oil (Hot Oil)

For those who love spicy food, chili oil is an indispensable condiment. Good chili oil is very hot, and only a couple drops are needed to perk up the taste of any dish. The variety made with sesame oil usually is not very strong. Available in Oriental markets; Tabasco sauce is an adequate substitute.

Chili Paste or Hot Pepper Sauce

This paste of very hot red chili with added salt and wine can be used in cooking or can be served as a condiment. It comes in cans or jars; the Szechuan or Cantonese styles are interchangeable. Handle with care—one should start with small amounts and taste carefully before moving to larger quantities. Frequently this ingredient seems to increase in potency after the dish is cooked and set on the table.

Chili Peppers, Fresh or Dried, Red or Green

Chili peppers come in many varieties, all of which are very hot. Usually the smaller ones are hotter, and when the seeds are left in, the strength is increased. Always remember not to rub your eyes while handling them. If dried ones are used, they should be soaked in hot water for half an hour before using. Canned Mexican red chilis can be substituted.

Chinese Cabbage or Napa Cabbage

There are two varieties of this vegetable. One is thin and long, with stalks tightly packed together. The other is rounder, plumper, and slightly shorter. Both varieties can often be found in larger supermarkets, and they are interchangeable in all recipes. A whole head is usually too much to use for one meal, so seal the remaining part in a plastic bag, where it will keep for a couple of weeks when stored in the refrigerator.

Chinese Chives

A member of the onion family, Chinese chives impart a mild garlic flavor. A perennial, they are available from early summer until late August. The stems are ¼ inch wide, flat, and much darker in color than regular chives. They need a very short cooking time and are delicious as an herb in soups or when cooked with bean curd. The Chinese often stir-fry a large quantity and serve it as a vegetable. Chinese chives can be grown easily indoors or out. When stems reach a height of about 10 inches, cut them off and a new crop will start. Store chives in a sealed plastic bag; they will keep for one week in the refrigerator.

Chinese Mustard Greens

A dark green vegetable with ruffled leaves and thick stems loosely wrapped into a head. It has a slightly bitter taste. Delicious in soups or cooked with fermented black beans and garlic. (See Chinese Mustard Greens in Black Bean Sauce, page 173.) Available in some supermarkets; grows easily in any type of soil.

Chinese Okra or Luffa Squash

A very tasty green squash; it is long and thin with a grooved surface resembling a giant okra. Because of its delicate taste it is used to enrich soups and heighten the flavor of other vegetables. Large-sized ones are dried and peeled and used as sponges in the bath.

Chinese Parsley or Fresh Coriander
An aromatic herb with a strong, distinctive flavor. Its leaves are serrated and resemble those of chervil. Available in Chinese grocery stores or in supermarkets that sell Spanish and Mexican ingredients. Usually comes with the root intact; should be stored in the refrigerator in a sealed plastic bag without rinsing or removing the roots. It is easy to grow fresh coriander at home; just plant ordinary coriander seeds either indoors or outdoors and they will grow very rapidly.

Chinese Turnips
See *Radish, Chinese.*

Cloud Ears
See *Tree Ears.*

Eggs, Salted
These come coated with a dark claylike paste. They are duck eggs soaked in salted water for a couple of months, then preserved in ashes. The whites tend to taste saltier than the yolks. Delicious when cooked with fresh eggs. The Cantonese use the yolks as delicacies.

Eggs, Thousand-Year, Ming Dynasty, or Century Eggs
Thousand-year eggs are preserved by coating duck eggs with a mixture of ashes, lime, salt, and usually rice husks, then aging them in an earthen urn for a few months. When they are cured, the yolks become dark olive-green and have the consistency of Brie cheese; the whites are firm and gelatinous. The Chinese believe that well-aged eggs should have moist, running yolks and whites speckled with snowflake patterns; it is said that using ashes from pine tree needles produces these patterns. Thousand-year eggs usually are served as an appetizer with soy sauce, sesame oil, and pickled ginger. Prepare by scraping off the ash mixture, removing the shell, then cutting each egg into lengthwise sections. They can also be cut up and cooked with fresh eggs.

Fermented or Salted Black Beans
A Cantonese specialty, fermented black beans are often used

with garlic; both ingredients give a strong, distinctive flavor to dishes and should be used sparingly. Fermented black beans come in cans and plastic bags, and, once opened, should be transferred to a covered jar and stored in the refrigerator, where they will keep for months.

Fish Sauce
A thin brownish sauce, very strong and salty, made by extracting juice during the fermentation of salted fish. A small amount added to vegetables lends a very special flavor.

Five-Spice Powder
A reddish brown combination of five or sometimes six different ground spices including star anise, cloves, cinnamon, fennel, Szechuan peppercorns, and ginger. It is popularly used in Shanghai cooking to flavor meat dishes and pressed tofu, and sold in bottles or in plastic bags. It should be kept in a tightly sealed jar.

Ginger Root
An essential ingredient in Oriental cooking, ginger root grows in knotty, conjoined bulbs that look very much like iris rhizomes and has a pungent taste and refreshing aroma. It's used sliced, shredded, or minced. When buying ginger, select a plump chunk with smooth, shiny skin. Do not wash ginger; just scrape the skin off the portion that is needed and store the remaining part without wrapping in the vegetable compartment of the refrigerator, where it will keep for a couple of months. The skin may shrivel up but the taste will still be fresh. For full flavor, ginger should be sliced paper-thin or cut into fine slivers. When minced ginger is called for in a recipe, first cut the ginger into thin slices, then mash the pieces with the blunt side of the cleaver, and finally chop with the sharp edge. Ginger is quite easy to obtain nowadays and is available not only in Oriental grocery stores but often in supermarkets as well.

Gingko Nuts
Fresh gingko nuts have a hard white shell and soft, ivory-colored meat. In the center of each nut there is a bitter greenish sprout which should be removed before using. Since canned

gingko nuts have been soaked in water for a long period of time, enough of the bitterness has been washed out so that the sprouts can be left in. Gingko nuts are not crunchy like most nuts; they have the texture of an olive and are slightly chewy. The Chinese use them in elegant vegetarian dishes, such as "Lo Han Vegetable Dish" (page 169), and also put them in sweet soups. Both the Chinese and the Japanese like to eat roasted fresh gingko nuts as an appetizer.

Gluten, Wheat (Also called Vegetable Steak)
(See page 165.)

Gwei Hwa
The flower of the cassia tree, tiny, sweet-smelling yellow blossoms. They are usually preserved in salt or sugar and used in pastries and sweet desserts. Available in some Chinese grocery stores.

Hoisin Sauce
A sweet reddish brown sauce with a creamy consistency like catsup. It is a mixture of flour, soybeans, garlic, sugar, salt, and chili and can be used as a condiment or for cooking. Hoisin sauce is sold in cans or in jars; I prefer the canned variety. If transferred to a covered jar, it will keep for a long time in the refrigerator.

Litchees
Fresh litchees, a specialty of Kwangtung Province, grow in clusters on trees and have a rough, reddish brown skin that should be peeled off and discarded. The fruit inside is white, very sweet, and has the consistency of a grape; the ones with single small pit are the best. Litchees are also grown in Hawaii and Florida. Peeled and canned litchees are sold in the gourmet section in supermarkets, but cannot compare to the sweet, delicate, juicy fresh ones. Many people consider litchees one of the world's most wonderful fruit.

Lotus Roots
The lotus, a water plant that grows in ponds, has been highly praised by Chinese scholars and poets. The plant grows out of

dark muddy water yet the straight stem and white flower stay clean and pure. Technically rhizomes, lotus roots grow horizontally under the soft mud of ponds. There are nodes separating each section of the root and hollow cavities run their entire length; when a cross section is cut, one can see many small holes. In some dishes these holes are stuffed with rice. The young roots can be eaten as fruit; they have the texture of an apple.

Melon, Winter

This pumpkin-sized melon is a kind of squash. It does not have much flavor of its own but picks up that of any flavorful ingredient with which it is cooked. The skin is green and coated with a white powderlike layer that should always be scrubbed off before cooking. The meat has a soft, smooth texture, is good for soups, and is also delicious when braised with soy sauce or spicy ingredients. It is usually sold, cut up, by weight—not by the whole melon, and is obtainable in Chinese grocery stores or some larger supermarkets. If it is wrapped loosely with a piece of plastic it will keep for a week in the refrigerator. If the surface becomes soft or bruised, cut off that portion.

Mung Bean Sheets

Mung bean sheets, like mung bean noodles, are made from mung bean flour. They come in thin round sheets about 10 inches in diameter. Only dried ones are available in the United States; they have a smoky gray color and are very brittle. After soaking they become slippery and have a chewy texture.

Mushrooms, Dried Chinese or Dried Black

An elegant ingredient in Chinese cooking, they rank as high in prestige in Chinese cooking as do truffles in French dishes. There are many varieties of dried Chinese mushroom; the most common ones available in the United States come from Japan. Dried mushrooms are rated by size; the larger and thicker the more costly. They should be stored in a cool place or wrapped tightly and kept in the refrigerator. They must be soaked in warm water before being used.

Mushrooms, Straw or Grass

Only canned and dried straw mushrooms are sold in the United States. Canned ones have a crunchy texture and are used in stir-fried dishes. The dried ones are generally used in soups.

Noodles, Mung Bean, Cellophane, Vermicelli, Bean Thread, or Transparent

Made from mung bean flour, these range in size from thin as a thread to thick as a string. They are packaged in 2- to 8-ounce skeins and are commonly used in stir-fried dishes, soups, and salads. Always sold dried, they become soft and translucent when cooked.

Noodles, Dried Rice Stick

This is a specialty of Fukien Province. Made of rice flour the noodles are thin, brittle, and opaque white, and are sold dried in 1-pound packages tied in 8-inch looped skeins.

Noodles, Fresh Rice

This kind of noodle is the favorite of the Cantonese; the name for it in Cantonese is "sa-haw-fun." It is made by pouring a ¼-inch thick layer of rice batter onto a large flat surface and steaming it until it becomes solid, then cutting the sheet into ½-inch wide strips. Available in Chinese noodle shops and grocery stores, it also comes in dried form, but this is not a very satisfactory substitute for fresh.

Oyster Sauce

A rich thick sauce made of oysters, soy, and brine. It has a wonderful delicate flavor that gives zest to subtle or bland dishes. Store in the refrigerator after opening.

Radish, Chinese, or Chinese Turnips

A Chinese radish resembles a giant icicle radish and is quite similar in taste. The Chinese name is lo-bo; the Japanese is dai-kon. Available in larger supermarkets and Oriental grocery stores.

Red-in-Snow or Pickled Mustard Greens

This is a salty pickled vegetable made with what the West calls mustard greens. It is a bit bitter when cooked fresh, but the pickled variety has a divine taste. Red-in-snow adds a nice flavor to soups and to vegetables. It is available in large and small cans, but buy the small one if possible. If you transfer the unused portion to a covered jar, it will keep up to two months in the refrigerator.

Rice, Glutinous or Sweet

A short-grain rice of milky white color that becomes sticky when cooked. Used mostly for sweets.

Seaweed or Dried Laven Sheets

Comes in purplish paper-thin sheets that are made by pressing together certain parts of a species of marine plant. The Japanese and Korean products are usually packed in a plastic bag containing 10 sheets, each about 8 inches square. Chinese ones are generally round and about 6 inches in diameter; sometimes the sheets are quite sandy. All three types are available in Oriental grocery stores.

Seaweed, Hair

A kind of seaweed that looks like fine black hair and has a very crunchy texture. Absorbs any flavor from the dish it is cooked in. Can be obtained in Chinese grocery stores.

Sesame Oil

An aromatic oil made from roasted sesame seeds. It is light brown in color. The pale-colored variety sold in supermarkets is not processed the same way and cannot be used in recipes calling for sesame oil. Available in Oriental grocery stores.

Sesame Paste

Made from ground sesame seed, sesame paste comes in cans and jars and looks like unhomogenized peanut butter. Once opened, it should be kept in the refrigerator to prevent it from becoming rancid. Stir and blend evenly before each use to rehomogenize it. Peanut butter can be substituted for sesame paste, but it does not have the same rich flavor. Available in Oriental grocery stores or health food stores.

Shao-Sing Wine or Chinese Rice Wine
Light brown in color, this wine is made from rice and contains about 14 percent alcohol. It can be purchased from Chinese liquor stores and also from some regular liquor stores. Shao-sing wine can also be served as a drink when slightly heated. Japanese sake is an excellent substitute; when it is impossible to get either, use a dry sherry.

Snow Peas
A special kind of pea that can be eaten whole—pod and all. They have a bright green color and are picked before the peas have matured. Available fresh or frozen in Oriental grocery stores and supermarkets.

Soy Sauce
This most essential seasoning comes in many varieties. In this cookbook the amount used in each recipe is based on an all-purpose soy sauce such as the Japanese brand Kikkoman, available in most supermarkets.

Soy Sauce, Light or Thin
Much lighter than Japanese all-purpose soy sauce, this is used mostly for more delicate and subtle dishes. If it is impossible to obtain light soy sauce, substitute Japanese all-purpose soy sauce.

Star Anise
This pretty herb looks like a star with eight corners and has a licorice-like flavor; it is related to the magnolia family. It is sold dried in Oriental grocery stores, and will keep indefinitely if stored in a sealed container.

Szechuan Peppercorns
A reddish brown, mildly spicy aromatic pod that has a tiny black seed, about the same size as a regular peppercorn. Most Chinese grocery stores carry them. Store in a sealed container.

Szechuan Preserved Vegetable (Ja-Tsai)
A salty, spicy pickle made from a kind of vegetable that grows in clusters of knobby stems. Sold in cans; once opened, it should be transferred to a clean covered jar and refrigerated. Will keep for months.

Tien-Tsin Preserved Vegetable
This is cut-up Chinese cabbage that has been cured with salt, sugar, garlic, wine, and ginger. It comes in a very attractive earthen crock. Once opened, it should be covered and kept in the refrigerator where it will keep indefinitely.

Tiger Lily Buds or Golden Needles
These dried lily flower buds are tan in color and have a slightly crunchy texture. They are used extensively in vegetarian cooking and should not be over-soaked, as they will lose their nutritive value.

Tree Ears, Cloud Ears, or Wood Ears
A crunchy-textured fungus that grows on dead tree bark. When fresh it resembles human ears, hence the name tree ears or wood ears. Also named cloud ears because most of this kind of fungus comes from Yunan Province ("yun" means "cloud" in Chinese). Sold by weight in Chinese grocery stores. Will keep indefinitely.

Tree Ears, White or Snow
This type of tree ears is creamy white in color and is considered a great delicacy in Chinese cooking.

Water Chestnuts
This ingredient is well known in the West. Water chestnuts are tubers of a plant that grows in marshes, and are dark brown in color with thin but tough skins. When peeled, the flesh is white, crisp, and sweet. Young water chestnuts are usually eaten raw as a fruit; more matured ones are used in cooked dishes. Peeling water chestnuts is very time-consuming; the canned ones, available at supermarkets, are perfectly good for cooking and save time.

STOCK

Stock is the key to all successful Chinese cooking. It is the secret ingredient which lends that mysterious and delicate flavor to many Chinese dishes. And a good broth is even more essential for cooking vegetable dishes than for meat dishes. Most vegetarian dishes have their own definite characteristics; still, the original taste of vegetables is quite subtle, and, when cooked alone, the natural flavor may not be very distinctive. Adding a small amount of sweet broth to the vegetables helps bring out the goodness of each ingredient and thus enhances the flavor of the dish.

A basic authentic Chinese vegetarian stock is prepared by simmering soybean sprouts or soybeans in water with one or two kinds of dried mushrooms and fresh chestnuts for a few hours. Vegetables such as leeks, cabbage, celery, potatoes, and carrots can be added to enrich the flavor of the stock, but this is inauthentic from the Chinese point of view. Onions, broccoli, Brussels sprouts, turnips, and the like are too strong for Chinese vegetarian broth. Soft vegetables such as tomatoes and zucchini will cloud up the stock too much. Lentil beans make tasty stock, but again, they generate too much sediment for use as broth. Soybeans or soybean sprouts have a delicate flavor and are most suitable for making stock. Soybean sprouts are much larger than mung bean sprouts and have a more chewy texture. They have a very sweet, delicate taste, and they are often used to strengthen the flavor of a dish. Two stock recipes are provided on pages 90 and 91.

Vegetarian bouillon cubes and mixes are very good substitutes when you are in a rush. Dissolve the cubes according to directions; there is no need to strengthen or dilute the flavor. Herb-Ox vegetarian bouillon cubes are available in supermarkets; Instant Vege-base mix and Swiss-made Morga and Hügli bouillon cubes can be obtained from health food stores. If it is possible, use bouillon cubes instead of Instant Vege-base for all the recipes in this book, because there is too much sediment in Instant Vege-base.

SALADS AND COLD DISHES

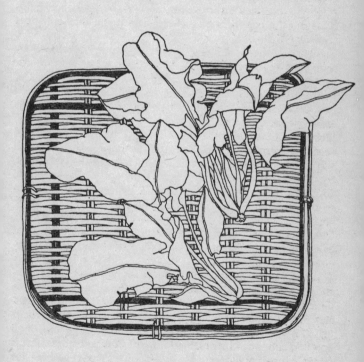

*There are plenty of exotic foods to nourish
the body but a vegetarian diet
provides better health.*

—*Chinese folk saying*

The Chinese have no tradition of eating vegetables raw. Leaf lettuce is the only kind of greens that they will occasionally eat without cooking. Other vegetables such as lotus roots and water chestnuts are also sometimes eaten raw as fruits. I nevertheless use the word "salads" for this section because most of the vegetable dishes included here are mixed with a sauce and served cold. They are very much like Western salads, except the vegetables are first blanched slightly in boiling water. They are all very delicious and can be served with Western-style meals as well as Chinese.

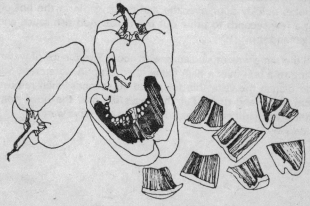

拌 WATERCRESS SALAD
西 WITH GARLIC SAUCE
洋
菜　If you have never tasted cooked watercress before, this
　　 dish is a good introduction to it. It is simple to prepare,
　　 has a very refreshing taste, and goes well with a bowl of
rice or a steak. If fish sauce is impossible to obtain, substitute
Kikkoman all-purpose soy sauce.

Spinach can also be served in the same way. Be sure to wash
spinach thoroughly and then break any large leaves into small
sections.

> 2 large bunches watercress
> 2 Tbsps oil
> 1 tsp minced garlic
> 1 Tbsp fish sauce
> 1/8 tsp sugar

Wash watercress thoroughly. Break into 2-inch pieces.

Place garlic in a serving bowl. Heat oil in a wok or a saucepan
over a moderate flame. When oil is very hot and starts to
smoke, quickly pour over the garlic. Stir garlic in the hot oil
for a few seconds to bring out the flavor. Add fish sauce and
sugar and stir.

Fill the same wok or saucepan with about 5 to 6 cups of water.
Bring to a boil over a high flame, then drop in watercress. Stir
and blanch the vegetable for about 30 seconds; then remove
from water and drain. Put the vegetable into the bowl containing the garlic sauce; mix thoroughly and serve warm.
Serves 4

五 FIVE-SPICE
香 PEANUTS
花
生

Cooked peanuts taste very different from the roasted ones. The Chinese often use peanuts in their cooking, especially for soup dishes. Try to use larger peanuts for this dish, and if possible get the ones with the skin on. Serve as an appetizer with drinks or just leave a plate of them on the dining table and let your guests test their chopstick skills.

You will notice that only one spice—star anise—is used here, despite the name of the dish. Dishes cooked with star anise often have the term "five-spice" in the title, even though less than five spices are used.

> 1 cup raw shelled peanuts
> 1 tsp salt
> 1 Tbsp star anise

In a saucepan, cover peanuts with 3 cups water, mix in salt, and add star anise. Cover pan and bring the water to a boil. Lower the flame and simmer for 30 minutes.

Uncover pan and drain off water. Discard star anise and pour peanuts onto a serving plate. Serve warm or cold.
Serves 4

涼拌乾絲 MIXED PRESSED BEAN CURD THREADS

In this dish bean curd threads give a meaty texture, red-in-snow contributes the delicate taste, and the sesame oil provides the fragrant aroma—altogether a wonderful harmony of ingredients. An ideal dish to star at a meal, it can be prepared ahead of time and should always be served at room temperature.

When bean curd threads and pressed bean curd are impossible to obtain or are too troublesome to make, substitute er-ju bean curd sheets (see page 50). Soak 12 pieces in warm water for 15 minutes, drain and cut into noodle-like strips. (Omit baking soda when er-ju bean curd sheets are used.)

> ½ tsp baking soda
> 6 oz pressed bean curd threads or 2 squares plain pressed bean curd or 12 pieces er-ju bean curd sheets
> 1 Tbsp light soy sauce
> ¼ tsp salt
> ¼ tsp sugar
> ½ Tbsp sesame oil
> 2 Tbsps chopped red-in-snow (pickled mustard greens)

In a mixing bowl, dissolve baking soda in 4 cups boiling water. Soak bean curd threads in the solution for 3 minutes. (If pressed bean curd squares are used, slice each square into thin slices, then cut the slices into very fine slivers.) Drain bean curd threads in a colander.

In a small bowl mix light soy sauce, salt, sugar, and sesame oil.

Mix drained bean curd threads and the sauce together. Mix in the red-in-snow, and place bean curd threads on the serving plate and serve at room temperature.
Serves 4

涼拌菠菜 SPINACH SALAD

When spinach is cooked properly, it is the tastiest of vegetables. Always remember to remove the spinach promptly from the hot water. Five-spice pressed bean curd can be omitted if you wish.

    10 oz fresh spinach (usually one package)
     1 square five-spice pressed bean curd (commercial or
        see recipe, page 122)
     1 Tbsp soy sauce
    ¼ tsp salt
    ½ tsp sugar
     2 tsps sesame oil

Wash spinach in cold water and drain. Blanch spinach in 6 cups boiling water for about 10 seconds, pour off hot water, and rinse spinach in cold water until vegetable is cool. Drain in a colander.

Cut pressed bean curd into thin pieces, then chop very fine.

Cut or chop spinach into small pieces. Squeeze out excess water with your hands and put chopped spinach in a mixing bowl.

In a small bowl mix soy sauce, salt, sugar, and sesame oil together.

Combine chopped spinach and chopped pressed bean curd together; then add the soy sauce mixture and mix thoroughly. Place on a serving plate, and serve at room temperature.
Serves 4

油豆腐拌菠菜 SPINACH AND DEEP-FRIED BEAN CURD PUFF SALAD

Another spinach dish with a richer texture. Er-ju bean curd sheets can be substituted for deep-fried bean curd puffs; soak 6 er-ju bean curd sheets in warm water for 15 minutes and cut into strips.

    10 oz fresh spinach
     8 deep-fried bean curd puffs (see recipe, page 120)
     1 Tbsp soy sauce
    ¼ tsp salt
    ½ tsp sugar
    ½ Tbsp sesame oil
    ½ Tbsp vinegar (optional)

Rinse spinach thoroughly and drain. Blanch spinach in 6 cups boiling water for about 10 seconds; pour off hot water and rinse spinach in cold water until vegetable is cool; then drain in a colander. Chop spinach coarsely and set aside.

Put fried bean curd puffs in a large bowl. Soak in 4 cups boiling water for 10 minutes or until the water is cool enough for the hand to touch. Squeeze the oil out of the fried bean curd puffs by hand, and then rinse with warm water. Cut each one into ½-inch strips.

In a small bowl mix together soy sauce, salt, sugar, sesame oil, and vinegar (if desired).

Mix spinach and fried bean curd puffs together, add soy sauce mixture, and blend thoroughly. Put spinach salad on a serving plate and serve at room temperature.
Serves 4

COLD EGGPLANT SALAD

A very soothing salad to serve on a hot summer day. The eggplant should be torn by hand in order to obtain an uneven edge, which picks up more sauce than an edge cut by a knife.

1   eggplant (about 1 lb)
1   Tbsp oil
2   tsps minced garlic
2   Tbsps light soy sauce
¼   tsp sugar
½   Tbsp sesame oil
1   tsp minced ginger

Peel eggplant and remove stem. Cut lengthwise into two halves.

Place eggplant in a steamer or on a plate and steam over boiling water for 15 minutes or until it becomes soft. Remove from heat and let cool.

Tear the eggplant lengthwise into strips by hand. Arrange the strips on a serving plate.

In a small saucepan, heat the oil, add garlic, and cook for a few seconds. Remove garlic and oil from fire, add soy sauce, sugar, sesame oil, and ginger. Pour sauce over eggplant and serve at room temperature.

Serves 4

拌 COLD CELERY
芹 SALAD
菜

When you need a quick Chinese vegetable dish to fill your dinner menu, this is ideal. As with spinach, be sure to drain celery at once.

> 1 small bunch celery hearts or 6 large, tender
>   celery stalks with upper sections and leaves removed
> 1 Tbsp light soy sauce
> ¼ tsp salt
> ⅓ tsp sugar
> 1 Tbsp sesame oil

Cut stringy fiber from celery stalks. Wash celery under cold water.

Slice stalks into pieces 2½ inches long by ½ inch wide.

Bring 6 cups water to a boil in a large saucepan, add celery and parboil for about 20 seconds. Drain at once and rinse with cold water.

Put celery into a mixing bowl, add light soy sauce, salt, sugar, and sesame oil. Mix thoroughly.

Transfer mixed celery to a serving plate and serve at room temperature.

Serves 4

SOYBEAN SPROUT SALAD

This dish is a fine source of protein and vitamin C. It can be prepared in advance and should be served at room temperature.

- 1 Tbsp sesame seeds
- 1 lb soybean sprouts
- 2 Tbsps soy sauce
- ½ tsp sugar
- ¼ tsp salt
- 1 tsp sesame oil
- ½ tsp hot chili oil (optional)
- 1 Tbsp chopped scallion

Toast sesame seeds in an unoiled pan over a low fire until they turn golden. Cool, then crush the seeds with mortar and pestle, or wrap in waxed paper and crush with rolling pin. Set aside.

Remove the root tails from soybean sprouts. (Some people feel the work involved in this procedure is not worth the effort, but it enhances the flavor and texture and I highly recommend doing it.) Rinse thoroughly and drain. In a large pan, bring 8 cups water to a boil; drop in bean sprouts and blanch for 2 minutes. Remove bean sprouts from hot water, drain, and chop coarsely.

In a small bowl combine soy sauce, sugar, salt, sesame oil, and chili oil (if desired). Mix sauce with chopped bean sprouts, add scallion and sesame seeds, blend thoroughly, and serve.
Serves 4

BEAN SPROUT AND EGG THREAD SALAD

To increase the protein content of this dish, one can replace cucumber with er-ju bean curd sheets. Soak 8 er-ju bean curd sheets in warm water for 15 minutes and cut them into thin strips.

   2 cups fresh bean sprouts
   1 large egg
   1 Tbsp oil
   1 medium cucumber (or substitute er-ju shoots)
   1 Tbsp toasted sesame seeds
   2 Tbsps soy sauce
   1 Tbsp vinegar
   ¼ tsp sugar
   1 tsp dry mustard or ½ Tbsp prepared mustard
   1 Tbsp sesame oil

In a saucepan, bring 6 cups water to a boil then reduce heat and add bean sprouts. Stir bean sprouts in hot water for about 5 seconds. Then drain off hot water quickly and rinse bean sprouts with cold water. Drain in a colander and set aside.

Break egg into a bowl and beat until well mixed. Set a skillet over moderate flame, add ½ Tbsp oil and swirl around the skillet to coat the pan evenly. Pour ½ of the beaten egg into pan; quickly swirl the pan around so that the egg forms a thin sheet. Cook until egg is completely dry; remove to a cutting board. Repeat the same procedure using the rest of the oil and egg. Fold the thin egg sheets into 3 or 4 layers and cut into slivers.

Peel the cucumber and cut it crosswise into 2½-inch sections. Cut the outer part of sections into thin slices and discard the seeds. Shred the thin slices into slivers.

Mix shredded cucumber, bean sprouts, and egg slivers together and then pile on a plate. Garnish with toasted sesame seeds.

In a bowl mix soy sauce, vinegar, sugar, mustard, and sesame oil together. Pour sauce over vegetables and egg just before serving.

Serves 4 to 6

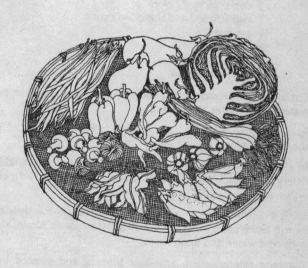

涼拌豆腐乾 PRESSED BEAN CURD SALAD

A perfect first-course dish, it is healthful and tasty without being filling.

1 cup soaked agar-agar threads (optional)
2 squares five-spice pressed bean curd (commercial or see recipe, page 123)
1 cup shredded celery
1 cup scraped and shredded carrot
¼ tsp salt
¼ tsp sugar
1 Tbsp soy sauce
1 Tbsp sesame oil

Cut agar-agar threads into 2-inch-long sections. Soak in cold water for 5 minutes, then drain.

Split each pressed bean curd cake into 3 thin slices and cut them into slivers.

In a saucepan bring 5 cups water to a boil. Drop in the shredded celery and blanch for 5 seconds. Drain, rinse quickly with cold water, and drain again.

Bring 4 cups of water to a boil again and drop in the shredded carrot; leave carrot in water for about 15 seconds. Drain, rinse with cold water, and drain again.

Combine celery, carrot, agar-agar threads, and pressed bean curd in a mixing bowl. Add salt, sugar, soy sauce, and sesame oil and mix thoroughly. Transfer everything to a serving plate, chill, and serve cold.

Serves 4 to 6

BEAN SPROUT AND MUNG BEAN NOODLE SALAD

1 oz dried mung bean noodles
1 Tbsp vinegar
2 Tbsps sesame paste or peanut butter
½ tsp salt
½ tsp sugar
1 Tbsp soy sauce
½ Tbsp sesame oil
½ tsp chili oil (optional)
4 cups fresh mung bean sprouts
1 Tbsp finely chopped scallion

Soak mung bean noodles in very hot water for 30 minutes. Drain and cut into 3- to 4-inch lengths.

In a small bowl, thoroughly mix vinegar, sesame paste, salt, sugar, soy sauce, sesame oil, and chili oil (if desired).

In a large sauce pan, bring 8 cups water to a boil. Drop in bean sprouts, blanch for 10 seconds, and drain. If the dish is not going to be served immediately, rinse bean sprouts with cold water until they cool and drain well. Set aside.

Combine mung bean noodles, bean sprouts, and scallion, then add the sauce and mix thoroughly.
Serves 4

SPICY CUCUMBER SALAD

1 large cucumber or 2 small ones
1 tsp salt
1 Tbsp soy sauce
½ Tbsp vinegar
½ tsp sugar
2 tsps chopped garlic
1 tsp chili oil or Tabasco sauce
½ Tbsp brown bean sauce (optional)
1 tsp Szechuan peppercorns
1 Tbsp sesame oil

Peel cucumber and cut it lengthwise into 2 sections. (If very small and tender cucumbers are used, leave the skin on.) Remove seeds with a spoon, then cut the outer part of the sections into pieces ¾-inch wide and ¼-inch thick. Put cucumber slices in a bowl, add salt, and toss thoroughly. Let stand for about 1 hour.

Wash cucumber with cold water, drain, and pat dry with paper towels. Combine cucumber with soy sauce, vinegar, sugar, garlic, chili oil, brown bean sauce, Szechuan peppercorns, and sesame oil and mix everything thoroughly. Marinate the cucumbers for at least 3 hours or overnight.
Serves 4

拌 CUCUMBER AND MUNG
粉 BEAN NOODLE SALAD
絲
黄
瓜

   1 oz dried mung bean noodles
   1 oz Szechuan preserved vegetable
   1 small cucumber
   2 Tbsps light soy sauce
   ¼ tsp sugar
   1 Tbsp sesame oil
   ½ tsp hot chili oil (optional)

Soak mung bean noodles in very hot water for 30 minutes. Drain and cut into 3- to 4-inch lengths.

Wash and soak Szechuan preserved vegetable in water for 10 minutes, then cut into very thin slivers.

Peel cucumber and cut it crosswise into 2½-inch sections. Cut the outer part of the sections into thin slices and discard the seeds. Shred the thin slices into very fine slivers.

In a small bowl, mix together light soy sauce, sugar, sesame oil, and hot chili oil (if desired).

Combine mung bean noodles, Szechuan preserved vegetable, and cucumber. Add the soy sauce mixture and mix thoroughly. Chill, and serve cold.

Serves 4

BRAISED MUSHROOMS

20 dried Chinese mushrooms, 1½ inches in diameter
(or 10 mushrooms, 2 to 3 inches in diameter)
1 Tbsp oil
2 Tbsps soy sauce
½ Tbsp sugar
½ cup unsalted vegetable stock
1 Tbsp sesame oil

Wash mushrooms and soak them in hot water for 30 minutes. Drain, and remove stems.

Set a small saucepan over moderate heat, add oil and mushrooms and stir for a few seconds. Add soy sauce, sugar, and stock. Cover pan and simmer mushrooms over low flame for 30 minutes.

Uncover pan, turn flame up to moderate, and boil mushrooms until the sauce is reduced to 2 Tbsps. Remove from stove and let cool.

Mix sesame oil with mushrooms. If larger mushrooms are used, cut them in halves. Arrange mushrooms attractively on plate and serve at room temperature.
Serves 4

豆芽卷 SPICY BEAN SPROUT ROLLS

　　1 Tbsp sesame seeds
　　1 lb fresh bean sprouts
　　4 sheets fresh or dried bean-curd sheet*
　　½ tsp hot chili oil
　　½ tsp salt
　　1 Tbsp chopped scallion
　　5 Tbsps oil
　　2 Tbsps sesame paste or peanut butter
　　2 Tbsps soy sauce
　　1 tsp sugar
　　1 Tbsp vinegar
　　1 tsp sesame oil
　　½ tsp Szechuan peppercorn powder (see recipe, page 168)

Toast the sesame seeds in an unoiled pan over a low flame until they become golden brown. Crush the seeds with mortar and pestle, or wrap them in waxed paper and crush with a rolling pin. Set aside.

In a large pan, bring 8 cups water to a boil. Drop in bean sprouts and blanch them for 10 seconds. Remove bean sprouts from hot water and immediately rinse them with cold water and drain. Squeeze the bean sprouts gently with your hands to remove excess water. In a bowl mix bean sprouts with ½ tsp hot chili oil, salt, and chopped scallion. Then add sesame seeds.

If dried bean curd sheets are used, soak them in warm water for 2 minutes and pat dry with paper towels. Spread one bean curd sheet on a flat surface, lay ¼ of the bean sprouts along the length of the sheet and shape them into a cylinder about

*Each sheet about 8 inches by 10 inches; if smaller sheets are used, increase the amount.

8 inches long and 1½ inches in diameter. Then roll up inside bean curd sheet like a jelly roll. Repeat, making 3 more rolls.

Set a skillet over a moderate flame and add the oil. When oil is hot, place the bean sprout rolls in the skillet and fry until they become golden brown on both sides. Transfer the rolls to a platter and cut them into 1-inch pieces.

In a small bowl mix sesame paste, soy sauce, sugar, vinegar, sesame oil, 1 tsp chili oil, 1 Tbsp water, and Szechuan peppercorn powder together. Pour the sauce over the bean sprout rolls and serve.

Serves 4 to 6

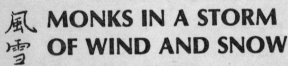 MONKS IN A STORM OF WIND AND SNOW

(Asparagus and Bean Curd Salad)

The imagery of this poetic title matches the contents of the dish: the tree ears represent the wind; mashed bean curd is the snow; and the asparagus stalks are the monks.

>   ½ cup soaked white tree ears
>   1 cup stock
>   1 tsp minced ginger
>   ½ Tbsp Shao-sing wine, dry sherry, or sake (optional)
>   2 squares fresh bean curd, 3 by 3 inches
>   ¾ tsp salt
>   1 tsp sesame oil
>   ½ Tbsp light soy sauce or regular soy sauce
>   ½ lb fresh asparagus
>   ½ Tbsp oil

Prepare tree ears as instructed on page 167. In a small saucepan, cover tree ears with ½ cup stock. Add ginger and wine and boil over a medium flame for 1 minute and drain.

Place bean curd in middle of a small piece of gauze, gather the edges and squeeze out excess water. Mix the now-mashed bean curd with ¼ tsp salt, soy sauce and sesame oil.

Snap off the tough end of each stalk of asparagus, rinse well and drain. Cut each stalk diagonally into 2-inch pieces. Heat oil in saucepan, add ½ tsp salt and the remaining ½ cup of stock. Boil asparagus uncovered in stock for 2 minutes and drain. Place asparagus in the center of a plate, surround with tree ears, then place bean curd on top of asparagus. Serve at once, or chill and serve cold.
Serves 4

⊞ SZECHUAN PICKLES

川
泡
菜

1 lb Chinese celery cabbage, or ½ lb cabbage and ½
    lb radish, or a mixture of cabbage, radish, cucumber,
    and carrot
2 Tbsps salt
2 slices fresh ginger
4 cloves garlic, crushed
½ tsp Szechuan peppercorn
1 Tbsp Shao-sing wine, dry sherry, or sake
2 or 3 red chili peppers, de-ribbed and cut into very
    small pieces

Wash vegetables and cut into 1-inch by 2-inch pieces. If radish
is used, cut into 1-inch by 2-inch by ¼-inch slices. Dry vegetables thoroughly with paper towels.

In a saucepan bring 4 cups water to a boil. Dissolve salt in
water, then add ginger and garlic; let cool to room temperature,
then add peppercorn and wine.

Place vegetables and chili pepper in a jar; pour in the saltwater
mixture. Cover jar tightly and let stand in the refrigerator for
3 days.

Drain pickled vegetables and serve cold.
Serves 4

CUCUMBER PICKLES

Most Chinese cold pickle dishes, such as this one, Spicy Cucumber Salad (page 78), and Szechuan Pickles (page 84), are served as side dishes with the main meal, and are not considered as one of the four or five main dishes. In banquet-style dinners, pickle dishes are nibbled as hors d'oeuvres before the actual dinner begins, and are placed on the table throughout the meal, as well as being served between courses to clear the palate for the next dish.

> 1 large cucumber or 2 small ones
> ½ tsp salt
> ½ tsp sugar
> 1 Tbsp soy sauce
> ½ Tbsp white vinegar
> ½ Tbsp sesame oil

Peel cucumber and cut in half lengthwise; with a spoon scoop out and discard the seeds. Cut the cucumber lengthwise into strips ¾ inch wide, then cut each strip diagonally into 2-inch lengths. Put cucumber in a bowl, add salt, and toss or mix thoroughly. Let stand for about an hour.

Rinse cucumber with cold water, drain, and pat dry with paper towels. In a bowl mix cucumber with the rest of the ingredients. The dish can be served right away, or can be marinated overnight before serving.
Serves 4

CANTONESE PICKLES

廣東泡菜

    1 large cucumber
    1 carrot
  12 oz giant radish or 10 icicle radishes
  ½ Tbsp salt
    2 Tbsps sugar
    3 Tbsps vinegar
    5 slices ginger

Peel cucumber and cut in half lengthwise; remove and discard seed. Cut the cucumber lengthwise into strips ½-inch wide, then roll-cut each strip diagonally into 1½-inch lengths.

Peel carrot and radish, and cut them into pieces the same size as the cucumber. In a large bowl, mix cucumber, carrot, and radish with salt and marinate for 2 hours. Rinse the vegetables with cold water, drain, and pat dry with paper towels.

Dissolve sugar in vinegar. Place cucumber, carrot, radishes, and ginger in a clean jar, then stir in the sugar and vinegar mixture. Cover jar and set in a cool place for at least 6 hours.
Serves 4

SOUPS

When hungry, vegetable soup, beans,
and corn can equal the taste
of rare dainties.

—Sung Dynasty poet
Su tung-p'o

The following section contains simple and easy-to-prepare soups of the type that usually accompanies family suppers. Only Mushroom Soup, Sizzling Rice and Straw-Mushroom Soups, and Mock Shark's Fin Soup belong to the banquet category. *Real* Shark's Fin Soup generally is considered one of the prestige courses at formal banquets.

Chinese soups can be served at any time in the course of a meal, at the beginning, in the middle, or at the end. At a family meal the soup is served at the same time as all the other dishes; usually the diners have small individual bowls and help themselves to a few spoonfuls of soup from the main soup bowl. Then they turn to the other dishes, sometimes returning for more soup or waiting until they are finished eating to wash down everything with a final bowl of soup.

In order to prepare a flavorful soup, good, fresh ingredients must be used. When preparing soup with ingredients like mung bean noodles or cucumbers, which do not have much flavor themselves, a good stock should be used. When tomatoes or preserved vegetables are in the recipe, plain water is sufficient. The two recipes that follow offer two methods of preparing the necessary rich vegetable stock.

SOYBEAN SPROUT STOCK

2 lbs fresh soybean sprouts
½ oz dried straw mushrooms (optional)
½ oz dried Chinese mushrooms
8 dried red dates (optional)
8 cups water
Salt

Wash bean sprouts in cold water several times and drain. Heat a wok over a high flame; when the wok is very hot, drop in bean sprouts. Stir and toast the sprouts in the dry wok for 1 minute or until the excess water is gone. Transfer bean sprouts to a saucepan.

Wash the two kinds of mushrooms with warm water, soak them in hot water for 30 minutes and remove stems. *Do not discard the mushroom water.*

In a large saucepan, combine together bean sprouts, mushrooms, mushroom water, red dates, and 8 cups water. Cover pan and set over a moderate flame. As soon as the water comes to a boil, lower the flame and simmer for 2 hours. Strain the stock with a piece of cheese cloth or a fine strainer. Season broth with salt to taste.

This recipe can be served as a soup dish by leaving all the ingredients in the liquid, adding ½ Tbsp sesame oil to the soup, and serving hot.

Serves 6 to 8

洋山芋上湯 VEGETABLE STOCK

When soybean sprouts are unobtainable, this vegetable stock is a perfectly good substitute.

1 lb potatoes
1 medium-sized carrot
4 stalks celery
4 scallions or 1 leek
4 cups water
Salt

Wash and scrub potatoes, carrot, and celery thoroughly. Cut potatoes into 2-inch chunks; slice carrot diagonally into thick ½-inch pieces; break each celery stalk crosswise into 2 or 3 sections. Rinse scallions or leek and remove roots, then cut each one in half crosswise. Place potatoes, carrot, celery, and scallion in a saucepan and cover with water. Bring everything to a full boil, then simmer over a low flame for 1 hour. Strain stock and season with salt to taste.
Serves 4 to 6

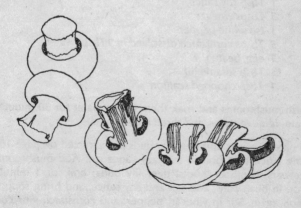

酸辣湯 HOT AND SOUR SOUP

This is the meatless version of a universally loved soup. Hot and Sour Soup originated in Szechuan Province and is considered very ordinary in China. The absolutely authentic version is a concoction of chicken blood, bean curd, bamboo shoots, tree ears, pork, eggs, vinegar, and pepper, garnished with chopped scallion and fresh coriander. Since the small amount of meat in the original version contributes little flavor, this vegetarian version is every bit as tasty.

    4 dried Chinese mushrooms
    1 Tbsp dried tree ears, soaked and washed
    ½ cup soaked tiger lily buds, cut
    4 cups stock
    ½ cup bamboo shoots, shredded
    1 cup fresh bean curd, cut into very thin pieces
    ½ teaspoon salt
    1 Tbsp soy sauce
    3 Tbsps vinegar
    1 tsp white pepper
    3 Tbsps cornstarch dissolved in 5 Tbsps water
    1 egg, beaten
    ½ Tbsp sesame oil
    1 Tbsp chopped scallion

Wash mushrooms and soak them in hot water for 30 minutes. Drain, remove stems, and shred mushrooms.

Prepare tree ears and tiger lily buds as instructed on page 167. Bring stock to a boil in a heavy saucepan. Add mushrooms, tree ears, bamboo shoots, tiger lily buds; boil for 1 minute. Drop in bean curd, add salt and soy sauce, and bring soup to a boil again. Stir in vinegar, pepper, and cornstarch. Stir constantly until the soup is thickened.

Turn off heat. Stir in egg; wait a few seconds for the egg to set and then pour soup into a big serving bowl. Add sesame oil and sprinkle chopped scallion on top. Serve at once.
Serves 6 to 8

DEEP-FRIED BEAN CURD AND MUNG BEAN NOODLE SOUP

This soup is actually a meal in itself. It is generally eaten as a snack or a light supper rather than to accompany a meal. It is a native dish of Shanghai but is well loved by Chinese everywhere.

    2 oz dried mung bean noodles
   10 deep-fried bean curd puffs (see page 120)
    4 cups stock
    1 Tbsp chopped Szechuan preserved vegetable
   ½ tsp salt
    1 Tbsp light soy sauce
    1 tsp sesame oil
   ½ tsp chili oil (vary amount according to taste)

Soak mung bean noodles in very hot water for 30 minutes. Drain.

Put deep-fried bean curd puffs in a large bowl. Pour boiling water over them and let them soak until the water is cool enough to touch. Squeeze the oil out of the fried bean curd puffs by hand. Rinse them with warm water a couple of times. Cut each one in half.

In a saucepan bring stock to a boil over a moderate flame. Drop in mung bean noodles, bean curd puffs, and Szechuan preserved vegetable. Bring everything to a boil again and simmer for 1 minute. Transfer soup to a tureen, add salt, soy sauce, sesame oil, and chili oil, and serve.

Serves 4 to 6

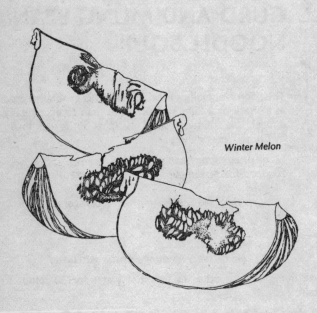

Winter Melon

冬
瓜
湯
WINTER MELON
SOUP

The Chinese believe that drinking winter melon soup in the summer will help to cool one's body temperature. Thus this soup is for summer.

> 1 lb winter melon
> 1 Tbsp Tien-tsin preserved vegetable
> 4 cups stock or water
> ½ tsp salt
> 1 tsp sesame oil

Remove seeds from melon and cut off the rind. Slice melon into pieces 1½ inches wide by 2 inches long by ½ inch thick.

Rinse preserved vegetable and drain.

In a saucepan combine stock and preserved vegetable. Bring stock to a boil over a moderate flame, add melon and cover pan. Boil slowly over a low flame for about 10 to 15 minutes. Season soup with salt and sesame oil. Transfer soup to a bowl and serve hot.
Serves 6

冬菇湯 MUSHROOM SOUP

This fine, rich, elegant mushroom soup is definitely for grand occasions. The preparations for this dish may seem complicated, but this traditional Chinese way of cooking delicate ingredients prevents the liquid from evaporating. The waxed paper is used for sealing in the steam. This dish can also be prepared with a double boiler or a crockpot. For more information, see the Steaming section in the Basics of Chinese Cooking, page 27.

    2 oz dried Chinese mushrooms
    2 thin slices fresh ginger
    1 scallion, cut in two crosswise
    3 cups stock
    1 Tbsp Shao-sing wine, dry sherry, or sake
    ½ tsp salt
    1 Tbsp light soy sauce
    1 tsp sesame oil

Wash mushrooms and soak them in 1½ cups hot water for 30 minutes. Drain; reserve soaking liquid. Remove stems and cut large mushrooms in half or thirds.

Place mushrooms in covered heatproof casserole, add ginger, scallion, mushroom liquid, stock, and wine. Seal the casserole top with waxed paper and cover it with the lid.

Place casserole on a rack in a pot large enough to hold it. Fill the pot with 2 to 3 inches of boiling water; cover pot with lid. Set the entire thing over a moderate flame and steam for 2 hours. Replenish steaming water every 30 minutes or when water goes below 1 inch.

Take casserole from pot, remove lid and waxed paper. Discard ginger and scallion; add salt, light soy sauce, and sesame oil. Serve hot.
Serves 4

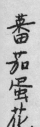

TOMATO EGG-DROP SOUP

This uncomplicated soup is pleasing to the eyes, comforting to the stomach, and easy on the wallet.

3 medium-sized tomatoes
1 Tbsp oil
2 Tbsps chopped scallion
½ teaspoon salt
3 cups stock or water
2 eggs, beaten

Soak tomatoes in very hot water for 5 minutes, or boil in water for a few seconds. Remove from water and peel off the skin. Dice the tomatoes.

Set a 2-quart pan over a medium flame and pour in oil. When oil is hot, add the chopped scallion and cook for about 20 seconds. Add the tomatoes and salt; cook tomatoes for 2 minutes or until they become soft. Add stock or water and bring to a rapid boil. Cover pan and boil soup over a low flame for about 5 minutes. Remove soup from the fire.

Uncover pan and stir in the egg slowly. Pour soup into a large serving bowl and serve hot.

Serves 4

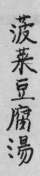

SPINACH AND BEAN CURD SOUP

This is a lovely soup, as spinach and bean curd make a perfect combination. Substitute 6 oz of cut-up watercress for the spinach and you have another delightful soup.

½ lb fresh spinach
1 square bean curd
4 cups stock
3 Tbsps cornstarch dissolved in ⅓ cup of stock or water
½ tsp salt
1 Tbsp light soy sauce
1 tsp sesame oil

Wash spinach thoroughly and break the leaves into small pieces; discard tough stems.

Rinse bean curd and dice.

In a saucepan bring stock to a boil. Add spinach and bean curd and simmer for 1 minute, uncovered.

Stir in dissolved cornstarch gradually. Cook until soup becomes thick. Season with salt, light soy sauce, and sesame oil, and serve hot.
Serves 4 to 6

SEAWEED AND BEAN CURD SOUP

Seaweed may not sound all that exciting to a Western palate, but do try it: you will be happy to discover its delightful taste and also add a healthy soup to your repertoire.

> 3 pieces seaweed sheets (dried laven sheets)
> 1 oz Szechuan preserved vegetable
> 4 cups stock
> 2 squares bean curd
> ½ teaspoon salt
> 2 Tbsps cornstarch dissolved in ¼ cup of stock or water
> ½ Tbsp sesame oil

With a pair of scissors cut seaweed sheets into pieces 1-inch square and set aside.

Wash Szechuan preserved vegetable with water and chop into small pieces.

In a saucepan combine stock and Szechuan preserved vegetable. Bring to a boil and then simmer for 20 minutes over a low flame.

Cut bean curd into 1-inch cubes and add to the soup. When the soup comes to a boil again, add salt and thicken soup with dissolved cornstarch. Stir in seaweed, then add sesame oil. Transfer soup to a bowl and serve hot.

Serves 4 to 6

黄豆湯 SOYBEAN SOUP

Some Shanghai restaurants specialize in Shanghaiese fast food. Most of the dishes are already cooked and served cold. The prepared foods are usually displayed on the counter in front of the restaurant, somewhat resembling the Spanish tapas that are served in bars and cafés. The diners are able to see what the menu is for the day and make a choice of any of these dishes. Piping hot Vegetable Rice (page 272) and Soybean Soup are the two principal items that go with these dishes; they are served automatically, without being ordered. To enrich the flavor of the soup, some pork bones are often added to the water. The semi-vegetarian can add a piece of blanched pork chop or a piece of soup bone and simmer with the beans. Remove and discard the chop or bone before serving.

> 1 cup dried soybeans
> ½ Tbsp Shao-sing wine, dry sherry, or sake
> 1 Tbsp light soy sauce (½ Tbsp if bouillon cube is used)
> ½ tsp salt (¼ tsp if bouillon cube is used)
> ¼ tsp sugar
> 1 small bouillon cube (optional)

Rinse soybeans. Without soaking put beans in a soup pot, add 5 cups water, then bring to a boil over high heat. Reduce flame to low, cover pan, and simmer for 3 to 4 hours. Stir in the rest of the ingredients and serve hot.

Serves 4 to 6

SOYBEAN WITH FRIED GLUTEN SOUP

This is a hearty soup that is high in protein. It can also serve as a snack.

    10 fried gluten balls, about 2 inches in diameter
    ½   cup dried soybeans
     4 cups stock or water
     6 fresh mushrooms, about 1 inch in diameter
    ½   tsp salt
     1 Tbsp light soy sauce
    ½   sesame oil

Prepare fried gluten balls as instructed on page 166.

Wash soybeans. Pick out and discard any foreign particles. Pour beans into a saucepan, add 4 cups stock or water and bring to a boil. Cover pan and simmer over a low flame for 3 hours.

Wash gluten balls in hot water to remove excess oil. Cut each one into 4 small pieces.

Rinse mushrooms and cut them into thin slices.

Add gluten and mushrooms to soup and boil for a couple of minutes. Season with salt, soy sauce, and sesame oil and serve hot.
Serves 4 to 6

CUCUMBER WITH MUNG BEAN NOODLE SOUP

2 oz dried mung bean noodles
2 oz Szechuan preserved vegetable
1 medium-sized cucumber
1 Tbsp oil
1 tsp Shao-sing wine, dry sherry, or sake
4 cups stock or water
½ tsp salt
½ Tbsp sesame oil

Soak mung bean noodles in very hot water for 30 minutes. Drain.

Wash Szechuan preserved vegetable, then cut into very thin slices. (Szechuan preserved vegetable is heavily salted and also spiced with chili pepper powder. If a milder taste is preferred, rinse it thoroughly and soak in water for 15 minutes before using.)

Peel cucumber and cut in two lengthwise. Scrape out the seeds with a spoon. Cut each half crosswise diagonally into 1 by 2-inch slices. If zucchini is used, follow same procedure.

Set a saucepan over a moderate flame, add oil, drop in cucumber. Stir cucumber in hot oil for about 1 minute. Add wine, then pour in stock or water and add Szechuan preserved vegetable. Cover pan and bring soup to a boil, then lower the flame and let simmer for 2 minutes. Uncover, add mung bean noodles, and boil soup for another minute. Add salt and sesame oil. Pour into a large bowl and serve hot.

For a variation, Zucchini may be substituted.
Serves 4 to 6

SPINACH EGG-DROP SOUP

1 Tbsp dried tree ears, soaked and washed
2 cups fresh spinach
4 cups stock
1 Tbsp soy sauce
½ teaspoon salt
1½ Tbsps cornstarch, dissolved in 2 Tbsps water
2 eggs, lightly beaten

Prepare tree ears as instructed on page 167.

Wash spinach thoroughly and drain. Break into small pieces and set aside.

In a saucepan bring stock to a boil over a medium flame. Add tree ears, spinach, soy sauce, and salt. Thicken the soup with dissolved cornstarch. Bring the soup to a boil again, then turn off flame. Pour in the egg and stir gently; as soon as the egg sets, transfer soup to a big bowl or a soup tureen and serve at once.
Serves 4 to 6

片
兜
湯

SPINACH AND NOODLE SOUP

This is a humble and earthy combination with everything thrown into one pot. Just the thing to serve with Scallion Pancakes (page 237) when you want something Chinese but simple. Generally it is considered appropriate as a light lunch or a between-meal snack.

        20 store-bought or homemade wonton wrappers
            (page 235), or
         1 cup dried wide noodles
         4 oz fresh spinach
         4 cups stock
        ½ Tbsp Tien-tsin preserved vegetable
         1 Tbsp oil
        ½ tsp salt
            Dash black pepper
         1 tsp sesame oil
            Chili oil (optional)

Cut wonton wrappers (if used) into strips about 1 inch wide.

Rinse spinach and drain. Break large leaves into smaller pieces.

In a saucepan bring stock to a boil over a medium flame, add Tien-tsin preserved vegetable, and simmer the stock covered for 2 minutes. Loosen wonton wrappers, making sure they are not stuck together, drop them into the soup, and boil for 2 minutes. Stir the soup a few times to prevent noodles from sticking to the pan. Add oil, spinach, salt, and pepper; when spinach becomes soft, stir in sesame oil. Pour into a soup bowl and serve. A few drops of chili oil may be added before serving. Serves 4 to 6

CURRIED CHINESE OKRA SOUP

Curry is of course an Indian contribution to Chinese cuisine; Chinese cooks have always been ready to adopt new ingredients and spices. Most of the Chinese curried dishes, however, bear no resemblance to the authentic Indian foods. Thus this dish is still authentic Chinese.

1 cup mung bean noodles
1 Chinese okra, about 8 to 10 oz*
1 Tbsp oil
1 tsp curry powder
4 cups stock
2 slices ginger
1 Tbsp Shao-sing wine, dry sherry, or sake
½ tsp salt
1 Tbsp light soy sauce

Soak mung bean noodles in very hot water for 30 minutes. Drain.

Cut off the hard stringy ends of the okra. Peel away a good part of the skin, but leave a few areas unpeeled to add color to the dish. Roll-cut into triangular pieces about 1½ inches long.

Heat oil in a saucepan over medium heat, stir in curry powder, and cook for 5 seconds. Add stock, okra, ginger, wine, and mung bean noodles, cover pan, bring soup to a boil, then simmer for 2 minutes. Season with salt and soy sauce. Pour soup into a large bowl and serve.
Serves 4 to 6
* For a variation, zucchini can be substituted for okra.

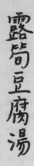

ASPARAGUS AND BEAN CURD SOUP

½ lb fresh asparagus or 1 cup defrosted frozen
    asparagus
1 Tbsp oil
½ Tbsp Shao-sing wine, dry sherry, or sake
4 cups stock
1 square fresh bean curd, diced
½ tsp salt
1 Tbsp light soy sauce
2 Tbsps cornstarch dissolved in 4 Tbsps water
1 egg white, slightly beaten
Dash white pepper
1 tsp sesame oil

Snap off the tough end of each stalk of asparagus, rinse the stalks thoroughly with cold water, and drain. Roll-cut each stalk diagonally into 1-inch pieces.

Heat oil in a saucepan over a medium flame, drop in asparagus stalks, and stir them in hot oil for 30 seconds. Add wine and stocks, bring to boil, and simmer uncovered for 2 minutes. Add bean curd, salt, and light soy sauce, then thicken soup with dissolved cornstarch. Gradually stir in egg white, and sprinkle with white pepper and sesame oil. Serve.

Serves 4 to 6

VELVET CORN SOUP

1 8-oz can creamed corn
4 cups stock
½ teaspoon salt
1 Tbsp cornstarch dissolved in 3 Tbsps water
1 egg white
1 Tbsp grated carrot

In a saucepan combine creamed corn and stock. Set pan over a moderate flame and bring slowly to a boil. Add salt, then thicken soup with dissolved cornstarch.

Beat egg white until fluffy and stir slowly into the soup. Quickly bring soup to a boil and remove from fire at once. Pour soup into a serving bowl, garnish with grated carrot, and serve.
Serves 4 to 6

西洋菜湯 WATERCRESS SOUP

2 bunches fresh watercress
1 Tbsp oil
4 cups stock
¼ cup shredded bamboo shoots (optional)
1 tsp salt

Trim off the tough part of the watercress stems and discard withered and yellow leaves. Wash watercress thoroughly and cut into 2-inch-long pieces.

Set a heavy pan over a moderate flame and add oil. When oil is hot, drop in watercress. Stir vegetable for 1 minute, pour in stock, and add bamboo shoots. Bring soup to a boil and let simmer uncovered for 10 minutes. Add salt and serve hot.

For variation, 1 beaten egg may be added at the very end of this recipe to make watercress egg-drop soup.

Serves 4 to 6

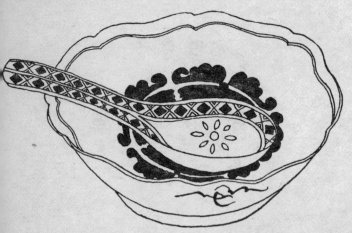

CHINESE RADISH SOUP

Although this is peasant soup, it is good enough to please the patrician palate.

½ lb Chinese white radish
¼ cup red-in-snow (pickled mustard greens)
1 leek
1 Tbsp oil
4 cups stock or water
½ tsp salt

Peel Chinese white radish; cut crosswise into ¼-inch-thick slices, each slice about 1 inch by 2 inches.

Rinse red-in-snow and chop finely. Wash leek thoroughly to remove the sand, and chop coarsely.

Set a soup pan over a moderate flame and add oil. When oil is hot, drop in leek and red-in-snow; stir in hot oil for 30 seconds. Add stock and radish, cover, and simmer for 30 minutes.

Uncover pan, season soup with salt, and serve hot.
Serves 4 to 6

SIZZLING RICE AND STRAW MUSHROOM SOUP

So-called because the moment the soup and the hot rice crust touch each other, they give out a sizzling sound. This last step should be done in front of the diners; it is fun to watch and also impressive.

½ cup canned straw mushrooms
5 cups stock
1 cup fresh mushrooms, sliced
¼ cup shredded bamboo shoots
1 tsp Shao-sing wine, dry sherry, or sake
1 tsp salt
1 Tbsp light soy sauce
1 tsp sesame oil
8 pieces of 2-inch crust (see recipe, page 274)
4 cups oil

Quarter each canned straw mushroom lengthwise and set aside.

Pour stock into a large saucepan. Add fresh mushrooms to stock, set over a moderate flame, and bring to a boil. Simmer for 2 minutes. Add straw mushrooms, bamboo shoots, wine, salt, and soy sauce. Bring soup to a boil again and remove from flame. Add sesame oil.

Heat oil in a wok or a deep fryer until very hot. Drop in the rice crust and fry until golden brown. Drain and put in a serving bowl.

Reheat soup and pour into a large bowl. Bring the fried rice crust and the soup to the dining table immediately. This should be done *quickly*, while both soup and crust are hot, to assure sizzling. Pour the soup over the rice crust and serve at once. Serves 4 to 6

MOCK SHARK'S FIN SOUP

Shark's Fin Soup and Bird Nest Soup rank in the highest position among Chinese soups. People go through great risk and effort to obtain shark's fins and bird nests, and the preparation of the soups is very time-consuming. Even after the shark's fin has been cleaned and processed, it requires cooking in three changes of rich chicken broth before being combined with the other ingredients. It is a tradition that at elaborate banquets the guest of honor must arrive before this soup can be served and may depart at any time afterward. As a vegetarian substitute for shark's fin, this recipe uses mung noodles; the consistency and flavor are amazingly similar.

> 5 medium-sized dried Chinese mushrooms
> 1 oz dried mung bean noodles
> 1 cup bean sprouts
> 1 Tbsp oil
> 5 cups stock
> ½ cup finely shredded carrot
> ½ cup finely shredded bamboo shoots
> ½ Tbsp Shao-sing wine, dry sherry, or sake
> 1 tsp salt
> 2 Tbsps light soy sauce
> 3 Tbsps cornstarch dissolved in ⅓ cup stock
> 1 tsp sesame oil

Wash mushrooms and soak them in hot water for 30 minutes. Drain, remove stems, and cut each mushroom into slivers. Set aside.

Soak mung bean noodles in very hot water for 30 minutes. Drain. With a pair of scissors cut noodles into 2-inch-long pieces.

Rinse bean sprouts with cold water and drain well. Set a wok over a high flame, add oil, and then bean sprouts. Stir-fry bean sprouts for 10 seconds and remove to a plate; spread bean sprouts apart and let cool.

In a large saucepan combine stock, carrot, mushrooms, bamboo shoots, mung bean noodles, and wine. Bring everything to a boil over a moderate flame, then lower the flame and simmer for 2 minutes. Add salt, soy sauce, and bean sprouts, and then thicken soup with dissolved cornstarch. Transfer soup to a big bowl, add sesame oil, and serve hot.
Serves 4 to 6

觀音音湯 GODDESS OF MERCY SOUP

(Bean Curd with Tiger Lily Buds and Tree Ears Soup)

The Goddess of Mercy, or Kuan-yin, is a Chinese incarnation in female form of a male Indian bodhisattva called Avalokitesvara. Chinese families traditionally petitioned Kuan-yin for the birth of sons. The ingredients here have no particular connection with the name of the dish, but the monasteries, where vegetarian dishes were common, often gave such poetic and religious-sounding titles to their food. Another example of this tendency is the Lo Han Vegetable Dish (see page 169); Lo Han is a term for a Buddhist who has attained enlightenment.

½ cup soaked and chopped tiger lily buds
½ cup soaked and chopped tree ears
1 square fresh bean curd
4 cups stock
2 Tbsps cornstarch dissolved in ¼ cup stock
½ tsp salt
2 Tbsps light soy sauce
1 tsp sesame oil
1 Tbsp chopped Chinese parsley

Prepare tree ears and tiger lily buds as instructed on page 167 and chop.

Rinse bean curd with cold water and dice.

In a saucepan bring stock to a boil over a moderate flame. Add diced bean curd, chopped tiger lily buds, and chopped tree ears. Bring to a boil and thicken soup with dissolved cornstarch. Add salt, soy sauce, and sesame oil. Sprinkle chopped Chinese parsley and serve hot.

Serves 4 to 6

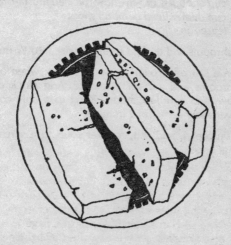

三
仙
湯 # THREE IMMORTALS SOUP
(Mushrooms, Red-in-Snow, and Bamboo Shoot Soup)

The Chinese word for "tasty" sounds identical to the word for "an immortal." Materials such as mushrooms, red-in-snow, and bamboo shoots are considered tasty ingredients; hence for this dish one single pronunciation serves a poetic and a descriptive purpose.

>   4 oz fresh mushrooms
>   1 Tbsp oil
>   4 cups stock or water
>   ½ cup chopped red-in-snow (pickled mustard greens)
>   ½ cup thinly sliced bamboo shoots
>   ½ teaspoon salt

Wash mushrooms and drain. Cut lengthwise into ¼-inch slices.

Heat oil in a saucepan over moderate flame; when oil is hot, add mushrooms and stir for 1 minute. Add stock or water, red-in-snow, and bamboo shoots. Bring to a boil, cover, and simmer over a low flame for 2 minutes.

Uncover saucepan, add salt, transfer soup to a serving bowl, and serve at once.
Serves 4 to 6

三
仙
會
東
海

THREE IMMORTALS AT THE EASTERN SEA

(Cream of Winter Melon Soup)

The characters for "east" and "winter" have the same pronunciation; hence the mashed winter melon that floats in this soup symbolically represents the Eastern Sea. Again, the three "immortals" are represented by the three "tasty" ingredients—mushrooms, carrots, and bamboo shoots.

- 1 lb winter melon
- 1 Tbsp oil
- 3 slices ginger, 1 inch in diameter
- 4 cups stock
- ½ cup shredded carrot
- 1 cup sliced fresh mushrooms
- ½ cup shredded bamboo shoots
- ½ teaspoon salt
- 1 Tbsp light soy sauce
- 1 Tbsp cornstarch dissolved in 2 Tbsps water
- 1 tsp sesame oil

Remove skin and seeds from winter melon and cut into thin slices. In a saucepan bring 3 cups water to a boil, drop in melon, and cook for 5 minutes. Drain and mash melon with a potato masher.

Heat oil in a large saucepan. Add ginger and cook for a few seconds. Then pour in the stock and add carrot, mushrooms, and bamboo shoots. Boil for 3 minutes. Add mashed winter melon and season with salt and light soy sauce. Stir in dissolved cornstarch, bring to a full boil, and add sesame oil. Serve hot. Serves 4 to 6

BEAN CURD DISHES, MOCK MEAT DISHES, AND MOCK FISH DISHES

The lasting pleasures are not in fine wine,
but in chewing beans and sipping water.

—Chinese folk saying

豆 BEAN CURD
腐

Bean curd is not just a necessity in Chinese vegetarian cooking, it is an indispensable food in the diet of the Chinese people. This unique ingredient is high in protein, yet low in cost. It is one ingredient that is relished by both rich and poor. It is a common dish at family meals, but it is also one that can be presented at a banquet.

Bean curd is made by softening dried soybeans in water, and then extracting the milk from the beans and coagulating the liquid with epsom salts, gypsum, or brine. Bean curd comes in several consistencies, which are used in accordance with the character of each dish. It can be purchased fresh or canned in cakes. It is available in Chinese or Japanese grocery stores, and can also be found in the Oriental section of some larger supermarkets.

It is also possible to make at home with the following recipe. Cover bean curd with water and store in the refrigerator, changing the water every other day.

> 1 cup dried soybeans
> 1 tsp epsom salts or 1 tsp gypsum

Rinse beans and soak in 2 cups water overnight. Drain beans. Put half of the soaked beans and 3 cups water into a blender. Blend at high speed until very smooth.

Spread a piece of gauze over a large bowl or a saucepan. Pour soybean milk over it and strain liquid into bowl. Gather the edges of the gauze and squeeze out the remaining milk. Discard the dregs.

Repeat this procedure with the rest of the beans.

Set soy milk in a pot over a moderate flame. Heat and stir until it comes to a full boil. Lower the heat and simmer for 2 minutes. Remove from flame.

Dissolve epsom salts or gypsum in ½ cup water. Stir the solution gradually into soybean milk. Pour the entire mixture into a perforated square cake pan lined with a piece of wet cheese cloth or gauze. Cover with a dishcloth and let stand undisturbed until it sets—about 30 minutes. Cut into 2-inch squares and gently float the squares by adding 1 cup cold water to the pan. If not for immediate use, cover bean curd with water and store in the refrigerator.

油 DEEP-FRIED BEAN
豆 CURD PUFFS
腐

Of the many and varied kinds of bean curd, deep-fried bean curd is the most versatile. It can be cooked with vegetables, added to soup, braised in sauce, stir-fried with eggs, mixed with salad, stuffed with any ingredients, or just served as an appetizer.

Since the deep-frying process extracts most of the water content from the bean curd, it becomes drier and more absorbent and picks up any flavor that goes into a dish with it. As a result, deep-fried bean curd is often the tastiest part of the dish. Deep-fried bean curd puffs are somewhat chewy and have a meaty texture and a very delightful, distinctive flavor.

The Chinese commercial deep-fried bean curd puffs are made of bean curd that is prepared differently from regular bean curd. After deep-frying the bean curd becomes very light and airy inside, and crisp golden brown on the outside. Chinese deep-fried bean curd puffs come in 1½-inch cubes. There are Japanese deep-fried bean curd puffs (age), which generally are very flat and come in square or rectangular shapes. They are interchangeable with the Chinese deep-fried bean curd puffs used in all the dishes in this book. When fresh deep-fried bean curd is impossible to obtain, canned Japanese deep-fried bean curd puffs can be substituted; but since they have been pre-seasoned, they should be rinsed thoroughly in warm water before using.

Deep-fried bean curd puffs also can be made at home with the following recipe. Homemade deep-fried bean curd puffs are generally not as light and airy as commercial ones but taste just as delicious. Deep-fried bean curd puffs will keep for a long time in the freezer when sealed in plastic bags.

> 6 to 8 squares fresh bean curd, about 3 by 3 inches each
> 2 cups oil

Arrange bean curd in single layer on a board or a flat surface, and place a cutting board over them. Set a heavy weight on top of board and let stand for 3 to 4 hours. Cut each square of bean curd vertically into 4 equal cubes and pat dry with paper towels.

Over a moderate flame, heat oil in a wok or deep-fryer to about 300°. Carefully drop in 6 to 8 cubes of bean curd and deep-fry slowly, turning them occasionally with tongs. Cook for about 15 minutes and drain. Repeat with the rest of the bean curd.

豆腐乾 PLAIN PRESSED BEAN CURD CAKES

Pressed bean curd cake is a firmer form of bean curd; its texture is somewhat like that of Monterey Jack cheese. It is made by removing most of the water from regular bean curd cakes, then flavoring them with soy sauce and spices. Pressed bean curd cakes are available in Chinese grocery stores or can be made at home with the recipes in this book. They should be kept in an unsealed plastic bag under refrigeration.

To make plain pressed bean curd cakes, wrap squares of bean curd separately with cheesecloth. Arrange them in a single layer on a flat surface, then cover with a wooden board. Place a light weight (about 5 pounds) on top of the board and let stand overnight. Unwrap bean curd cakes and refrigerate them.

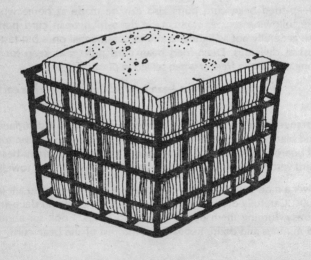

五 FIVE-SPICE PRESSED
香 BEAN CURD CAKES
豆
腐
乾

Five-spice pressed bean curd cakes are available at some Oriental grocery stores already prepared, but they can be easily made at home with the recipe below. They can be cut up into small pieces and served as an appetizer or stir-fried with vegetables.

½ cup soy sauce
1 tsp salt
½ tsp sugar
½ Tbsp star anise
¼ tsp five-spice powder
1½ cups water
4 squares plain pressed bean curd (2½ inches square)

In a saucepan combine soy sauce, salt, sugar, star anise, five-spice powder, and water. Simmer over a low flame for 10 minutes. Add pressed bean curd cakes to the liquid. Bring everything to a boil, then simmer uncovered very slowly for 5 minutes. Keep liquid just barely bubbling and never allow it to reach full boil. Remove from flame and soak pressed bean curd cakes in the liquid at least 4 hours. Drain and chill cakes in the refrigerator; save and refrigerate the spiced liquid for repeat use. When the stock becomes bland, replenish with the same amount of soy sauce and spices called for in recipe.

乾燒油豆腐 BRAISED DEEP-FRIED BEAN CURD PUFFS

To make this into an even richer dish, a cup of diced tomatoes may be added at the same time as the stock.

20 1-inch squares deep-fried bean curd puffs (see recipe, page 120)
 2 oz Szechuan preserved vegetable
 2 Tbsps oil
 2 Tbsps chopped scallion
 1 Tbsp soy sauce
 ½ tsp sugar
 1 cup stock
 ½ tsp sesame oil

Put deep-fried bean curd puffs in a large bowl. Pour 8 cups hot water over them and let soak until the water is cool enough to touch. Squeeze the oil out of the fried bean curd puffs by hand. Rinse with warm water a couple of times, then squeeze each piece by hand. Cut each one in two.

Rinse Szechuan preserved vegetable and chop. (If a milder taste is preferred, rinse vegetable thoroughly and soak in water for 5 minutes before using.)

Heat oil in a wok over a moderate flame. Stir in scallion and preserved vegetable and cook for about 20 seconds. Add soy sauce, sugar, stock, and fried bean curd puffs. Cover and simmer until most of the liquid is evaporated. Uncover and add sesame oil. Transfer to plate and serve hot.
Serves 4

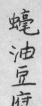

BEAN CURD WITH OYSTER SAUCE

A simple typical family dish usually served with rice. The Chinese believe that the smooth and velvety soft bean curd helps one swallow the grains of rice. The rich oyster sauce lends its flavor to the bland taste of bean curd, making a perfect balance.

3 squares fresh soft bean curd, 3 by 3 inches
2 Tbsps oil
2 Tbsps chopped scallion
2 Tbsps oyster sauce
1 Tbsp soy sauce
½ tsp sugar
Dash white pepper
½ cup stock
½ Tbsp cornstarch dissolved in 2 Tbsps water
¼ cup coarsely chopped fresh coriander (optional)
1 tsp sesame oil

Rinse bean curd and drain. Cut bean curd into pieces 1 inch square.

Set a wok or a skillet over high flame. Add oil, and when hot, stir in chopped scallion and cook for 20 seconds. Then drop in bean curd. With the spatula stir the bean curd gently; add oyster sauce, soy sauce, sugar, pepper, and stock; cook for 2 minutes. Mix well, then thicken sauce with dissolved cornstarch.

Turn off the flame and mix in chopped fresh coriander. Transfer bean curd to a bowl and serve hot with rice.
Serves 4

鍋塌豆腐 BRAISED BEAN CURD

4 squares fresh firm bean curd, 3 by 3 inches
2 eggs, beaten
5 Tbsps flour
3 Tbsps oil
2 Tbsps chopped scallion
1 tsp minced ginger
½ cup stock
½ tsp salt
1 Tbsp soy sauce
½ tsp sugar

Split each square of bean curd sideways in half, then cut into 1-inch by 2-inch pieces. Pat bean curd dry with paper towels.

In a bowl mix egg with flour to make a thin batter.

Set a skillet over a moderate flame; add 2 Tbsps oil. When oil is hot, dip bean curd in egg mixture and fry 6 to 8 pieces of bean curd at a time until both sides are brown. Transfer fried bean curd to plate. Repeat until all the bean curd is fried.

Pour remaining 1 Tbsp oil into still-heated pan. Add scallion and ginger and stir for a few seconds. Pour in stock, add salt, soy sauce, and sugar. Add the bean curd, cover skillet, and simmer bean curd slowly for about a minute. Transfer bean curd to plate and serve.
Serves 4

SPICY BEAN CURD

This dish is delightful in the wintertime. It is somewhat spicy, so when eaten with a bowl of hot rice it gives you extra warmth. (Of course, the aficionado eats it all year round.) Add a few drops of hot chili oil or ½ Tbsp of chili pepper paste if you like very hot food.

3 squares fresh soft bean curd, 3 by 3 inches
2 Tbsps oil
1 tsp minced ginger
3 Tbsps chopped scallion
1 Tbsp Szechuan hot bean paste
1 Tbsp soy sauce
½ tsp salt
½ tsp sugar
½ cup stock
½ Tbsp cornstarch dissolved in 2 Tbsps water
1 tsp sesame oil
¼ tsp Szechuan peppercorn powder (see page 168)

Rinse bean curd and drain. Cut bean curd into 1-inch-square pieces.

Set a wok over a high flame and add oil. When oil is hot, stir in ginger and 2 Tbsps scallion and cook for 20 seconds. Add hot bean paste and bean curd. With a spatula stir bean curd very gently. Add soy sauce, salt, sugar, and stock and bring everything to a full boil. Thicken sauce with dissolved cornstarch, then add sesame oil and peppercorn powder. Transfer the entire contents to plate, sprinkle with 1 Tbsp chopped scallion, and serve hot.
Serves 4

炒豆腐腦 STEAMED BEAN CURD WITH SPICY BEAN PASTE SAUCE

    3 squares fresh soft bean curd, about 3 by 3 inches
    2 Tbsps oil
    1 Tbsp chopped scallion
    1 tsp minced ginger
    1 tsp minced garlic
    1 Tbsp Szechuan hot bean paste
    2 Tbsps soy sauce
    ½ cup stock
    1 tsp cornstarch dissolved in 1 Tbsp water
    ¼ tsp Szechuan peppercorn powder (see page 168)
    1 tsp sesame oil
    1 Tbsp chopped fresh coriander (optional)

Steam bean curd for 10 minutes; drain. Cut into 1-inch squares, about ½ inch thick. Arrange neatly on a serving plate.

Heat oil in a wok or a skillet and stir in scallion, ginger, garlic, and bean paste; cook in hot oil for 10 seconds. Add soy sauce and stock and bring everything to a boil. Thicken the sauce with dissolved cornstarch, add sesame oil and Szechuan peppercorn powder. Pour the sauce over bean curd and garnish with coriander if desired.

An alternate method of cooking this dish is to omit step one, instead cutting the bean curd up into cubes and blending with the spicy sauce before adding the dissolved cornstarch.
Serves 4

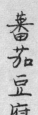

BEAN CURD WITH TOMATOES

Although tomatoes have been a part of Chinese cuisine for only about a hundred years out of the three millennia of its recorded history, today they are just as Chinese as the Great Wall.

2 medium sized ripe tomatoes
3 squares fresh soft bean curd, about 3 by 3 inches
2 Tbsps oil
2 Tbsps chopped scallion
½ tsp salt
½ tsp sugar
1 Tbsp light soy sauce or fish sauce
Dash black pepper
⅓ cup stock
2 tsps cornstarch dissolved in 2 Tbsps water
1 tsp sesame oil

Soak tomatoes in boiling water for 3 minutes, then peel; remove stems and seeds and cut into wedges. Cut bean curd into 1-inch by 2-inch pieces about ½ inch thick.

Heat oil in a wok or a skillet over a high flame and add scallion. Stir and cook in hot oil until slightly brown. Add tomatoes and cook for a minute, or until they become soft. Blend in bean curd, add salt, sugar, light soy sauce or fish sauce, pepper, and stock, and bring everything to a boil; then reduce heat and simmer for 1 minute longer. Thicken sauce with dissolved cornstarch and add sesame oil. Transfer to a serving plate and serve at once.
Serves 4

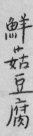

BEAN CURD WITH FRESH MUSHROOMS

    3 squares fresh soft bean curd, 3 by 3 inches
    ½ lb fresh mushrooms
    2 Tbsps oil
    2 Tbsps chopped scallion
    1 Tbsp oyster sauce
    1 Tbsp light soy sauce or regular soy sauce
    1 Tbsp Shao-sing wine, dry sherry, or sake
    ½ tsp sugar
    ¼ tsp salt
    Dash white pepper
    ½ cup stock
    ½ Tbsp cornstarch dissolved in 2 Tbsps water
    ½ tsp sesame oil

Cut bean curd into pieces 1 inch wide by 2 inches long by ½ inch thick.

Rinse mushrooms thoroughly, and cut into thin slices. Heat 1 Tbsp oil in a wok over a high flame, drop in mushrooms, and stir for 1 minute. Remove to a plate.

Heat the remaining oil in the wok. Add scallion and cook for a few seconds. Then add bean curd and all the rest of the ingredients *except* cornstarch and sesame oil. When the sauce comes to a boil, thicken it with cornstarch and add sesame oil. Serve hot.
Serves 4

拌豆腐 COLD BEAN CURD

This is a recipe for the true connoisseur of bean curd.

    2 squares fresh soft bean curd, 3 by 3 inches
    2 Tbsps soy sauce
    ¼ tsp sugar
    ⅛ tsp salt
    ½ Tbsp sesame oil
    1 Tbsp chopped red-in-snow (pickled mustard greens)
    1 tsp minced ginger

In a large bowl, soak bean curd in very hot water for 15 minutes. Drain well.

In a small bowl, mix soy sauce, sugar, salt, and sesame oil.

Place the bean curd on a serving plate. Cut each square into 6 small pieces.

Pour soy sauce over bean curd and garnish with chopped pickled mustard greens and ginger.

Serves 4

STUBBORN STONES' OBEISANCE

(Fried Bean Curd with Vegetables)

In this dish the bean curd cubes are deep-fried until the outside becomes firm and golden brown, but within the center remains soft. Hence the poetic name, suggesting hard but compliant rocks.

6 medium-sized dried Chinese mushrooms
3 squares fresh bean curd, 3 by 3 inches
½ teaspoon salt
½ lb bok choy or spinach
6 Tbsps oil
1 tsp minced ginger
½ Tbsp Shao-sing wine, dry sherry, or sake
2 Tbsps oyster sauce
1 Tbsp soy sauce
½ tsp sugar
Dash white pepper
⅔ cup stock
½ Tbsp cornstarch dissolved in 2 Tbsps water
1 tsp sesame oil

Wash mushrooms and soak them in hot water for 30 minutes. Drain, discard tough stems, and cut in two. In a small pan cover mushrooms with water and simmer over a low flame for 20 minutes. Drain.

Cut each bean curd square into quarters. Sprinkle salt over all sides of bean curd. Set aside.

Wash vegetable, removing any tough stems and wilted leaves. Separate the stalks and cut them into 3-inch long pieces.

Dry bean curd with paper towels. Heat 4 Tbsps oil in a skillet over a moderate flame. Brown bean curd in hot oil until both sides are golden (or heat 2 cups oil in a wok and deep-fry them). Remove browned bean curd to a plate.

Set a clean wok or a skillet over a medium flame. Heat 2 Tbsps oil, add ginger and the vegetable and cook for 30 seconds. Add mushrooms, wine, oyster sauce, soy sauce, sugar, pepper, and stock. Combine the ingredients thoroughly. Add the bean curd, dissolved cornstarch, and sesame oil. When the sauce becomes thick, transfer everything to a plate and serve hot.
Serves 4

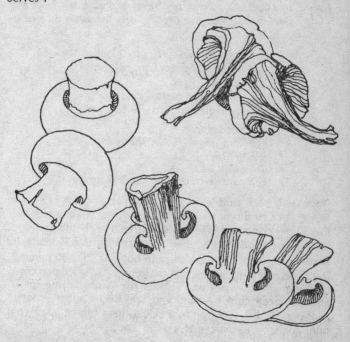

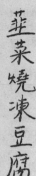

BRAISED FROZEN BEAN CURD WITH CHIVES

When bean curd is frozen the water is extracted. Upon defrosting a layer of concentrated vegetable protein is left. The texture is entirely different from fresh bean curd; it is somewhat chewy and spongy and picks up flavors instantly. This dish tastes even better when it is reheated, so make a big batch and save some for the next day. If leeks are used, add at the same time bean curd is added.

5 squares fresh bean curd, 3 by 3 inches
1 cup Chinese chives (or chopped leeks)
3 Tbsps oil
½ Tbsp brown bean paste
1 tsp minced ginger
⅔ cup stock
½ tsp sugar
1 Tbsp soy sauce
1 tsp sesame oil
½ Tbsp cornstarch dissolved in 2 Tbsps water

Place fresh bean curd in a square cake pan and put in freezer. When bean curd squares become frozen, run warm water over them until completely thawed again. Split each square into 2 equal halves horizontally, then cut each half into 4 triangular pieces.

Rinse Chinese chives thoroughly, then cut into 1-inch sections.

Squeeze bean curd by hand and remove as much water as possible. Heat 2 Tbsps oil in a skillet, then brown bean curd until golden, and remove to a plate. Pour remaining oil into a wok and add brown bean paste, ginger, stock, and fried bean curd. Bring sauce to a boil and cover and simmer over a low

flame for 5 minutes. Uncover, add chives, sugar, soy sauce, sesame oil, and cornstarch. Mix all the ingredients thoroughly until sauce thickens. Transfer to a plate and serve hot.
Serves 4

鹵豆腐 BRAISED FUKIEN BEAN CURD

In the original version this dish is simmered with a few ounces of lean pork to add more flavor to the bean curd; the meat and the sauce are then discarded.

> 4 squares firm bean curds, 3 by 3 inches
> 1 cup stock
> 1 Tbsp oyster sauce
> 2 Tbsps soy sauce
> 1 tsp sugar
> 1 Tbsp Shao-sing wine, dry sherry, or sake
> 2 scallions, each cut into 3 sections

In a saucepan, cover bean curd with cold water and boil over high heat for 10 minutes or until bean curd becomes full of holes. Remove from boiling water and drain.

Place bean curd in a saucepan and add stock, oyster sauce, soy sauce, sugar, wine, and scallions. Simmer over a medium flame for 20 minutes. Remove bean curd from sauce and slice into 1- by 2-inch rectangles about ½ inch thick. Serve with or without the sauce.
Serves 4

STIR-FRIED CHINESE CHIVES WITH PRESSED BEAN CURD

韭
菜
炒
豆
腐
乾

The mild garlic flavor of Chinese chives makes this a pleasantly pungent dish. One cup fresh mung bean sprouts may be added to the dish, or 2 cups substituted for the pressed bean curd.

    ½ lb fresh Chinese chives (or shredded leeks)
    2 squares five-spice pressed bean curd (see recipe, page 123)
    3 Tbsps oil
    1 Tbsp soy sauce
    ¼ tsp sugar
    ¼ tsp salt

Prepare five-spice pressed bean curd according to the recipe. Wash chives in cold water and remove wilted parts. Drain and cut off the tough white ends, then cut the chives into 2-inch sections.

Wipe pressed bean curd with a damp cloth. Cut each piece into slivers.

Set a wok or a skillet over a high flame. Add 1 Tbsp oil and then the pressed bean curd and stir-fry for 1 minute. Add soy sauce and sugar, mix evenly, and quickly transfer the contents to a bowl or a plate.

Pour the remaining 2 Tbsps oil into the wok or skillet. Add salt and then chives and stir-fry constantly over a high flame for about 30 seconds. Add pressed bean curd and stir all the ingredients quickly and thoroughly for 10 seconds. Remove to plate and serve at once.
Serves 4

STIR-FRIED PRESSED BEAN CURD WITH CARROTS AND BAMBOO SHOOTS

2 squares five-spice pressed bean curd (see recipe, page 123) or hundred-leaf bean curd sheets (bai-yeh), cut into thin strips

6 dried Chinese mushrooms
3 Tbsps oil
1 tsp minced ginger
½ Tbsp hoisin sauce
1 cup shredded carrots
½ cup shredded bamboo shoots or 1 cup fresh sprouts
½ Tbsp Shao-sing wine, dry sherry, or sake
2 Tbsps soy sauce
¼ tsp sugar
⅓ cup stock or mushroom cooking liquid
1 tsp cornstarch dissolved in 1 Tbsp water
1 tsp sesame oil

Prepare five-spice pressed bean curd according to the recipe. Wash mushrooms and soak in ⅓ cup of hot water for 30 minutes. Drain, remove stems, and cut into thin slivers. In a small saucepan cover mushrooms with the soaking water and simmer covered over a low flame for 15 minutes.

Heat oil in a wok or skillet, stir in ginger and hoisin sauce, and cook for 10 seconds. Drop in pressed bean curd or sheets, carrots, and bamboo shoots and stir-fry for 1 minute. Add wine, soy sauce, sugar, mushrooms, and stock, and toss and stir to mix everything thoroughly. Thicken with dissolved cornstarch, then add sesame oil. Transfer to plate and serve.
Serves 4

MOCK LION'S HEAD

素
獅
子
頭

Lion's head is a very popular dish among the Chinese. Simply pork meat balls on cabbage, it is a humble dish that never goes on the banquet table, but is nonetheless hearty and tasty. Here the meat is replaced by bean curd.

    1 square five-spice pressed bean curd (see recipe, page 123)
    4 squares fresh bean curd, 3 by 3 inches
    ¼ cup finely chopped water chestnuts
    2 Tbsps soy sauce
    1 tsp salt
    2 Tbsps flour
    ½ lb Chinese cabbage or bok choy
    ½ cup soaked tiger lily buds
    ½ cup soaked tree ears
    1 cup oil
    ½ cup stock
    ¼ tsp sugar
    1 tsp cornstarch dissolved in 1 Tbsp water
    1 tsp sesame oil

Prepare five-spice pressed bean curd according to recipe. Prepare tree ears and tiger lily buds as instructed on page 167.

Cut pressed bean curd into thin pieces, then chop very fine.

Wrap fresh bean curd in gauze and extract water by squeezing. In a large bowl mix the now mashed bean curd with water chestnuts, chopped pressed bean curd, 1 Tbsp soy sauce, and ½ tsp salt. Shape the mixture into 6 meatballs, and set aside.

Heat oil in a wok, deep-fry bean curd balls until golden brown. Remove and drain.

Rinse cabbage and cut into pieces 1 inch wide. Rinse them with flour. Then dust tiger lily buds and tree ears. Cut buds in half crosswise; break tree ears into coin-sized pieces.

Empty all but 2 Tbsps of oil from wok. Add cabbage, tiger lily buds, tree ears, and ½ tsp salt and stir-fry vegetables for 1 minute. Add remaining soy sauce, sugar and stock, and then place the bean curd balls on top. Cover and cook over a low flame for 10 minutes. Uncover and stir in dissolved cornstarch. Add sesame oil, then serve hot.

Serves 4

GREEN PEPPERS WITH MOCK MEAT

青
椒
妙
素
肉
絲

(Stir-Fried Green Peppers with Pressed Bean Curd)

Five-spice pressed bean curd is like cheese: you can always depend on it to give you a successful dish. Two cups fresh bean sprouts can replace pressed bean curd for a lighter and crunchier dish.

   2 squares five-spice pressed bean curd (see recipe, page 123)
   2 oz Szechuan preserved vegetable
   2 medium-sized green peppers
   3 Tbsps oil
   ¼ tsp salt
   1 tsp minced garlic
   ½ Tbsp Shao-sing wine, dry sherry, or sake
   1 Tbsp soy sauce
   ½ tsp sugar

Prepare five-spice pressed bean curd according to recipe.

Rinse Szechuan preserved vegetable and cut into thin slivers.

Cut peppers in half lengthwise. Remove seeds and rinse peppers well, then cut into thin slivers.

Split pressed bean curd horizontally into thin slices, then cut into slivers.

Set a wok over a moderate fire and add 1 Tbsp oil. When oil is hot, add salt and then the green peppers. Stir-fry for 30 seconds and transfer to a plate.

Pour the remaining oil into the wok. Add garlic and cook for a few seconds, then add pressed bean curd and Szechuan preserved vegetable and stir-fry for about 30 seconds. Add wine, soy sauce, sugar, and green peppers and blend all the ingredients thoroughly. Transfer to a plate and serve hot.

Serves 4

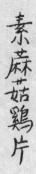

MOCK MOO GOO GAI PAN

(Stir-Fried Pressed Bean Curd with Vegetables)

    1 Tbsp dried tree ears
    1 cup fresh snow peas
    2 squares five-spice pressed bean curd (see recipe, page 123)
    2 cups fresh mushrooms
    4 Tbsps oil
    1 tsp minced garlic
    ½ tsp minced ginger
    ½ Tbsp Shao-sing wine, dry sherry, or sake
    1 Tbsp oyster sauce
    ½ tsp salt
    ⅓ cup stock
    ½ tsp sugar
    1 tsp cornstarch dissolved in 1 Tbsp water

Prepare tree ears as instructed on page 167.

Snap off both ends of each snow pea and remove the tough string on the sides. Rinse snow peas and drain.

Slice pressed bean curd into 1-inch by 1½-inch pieces.

Rinse fresh mushrooms in cold water, then pat dry with paper towels. Cut mushrooms into ¼-inch slices.

Heat 1 Tbsp oil in a wok over a high flame. Add snow peas and tree ears and stir-fry for 20 seconds. Remove to a plate.

Heat 1 Tbsp oil in the same wok and drop in pressed bean curd and stir-fry for 30 seconds. Remove to the same plate with the snow peas.

Pour final 2 Tbsps oil in wok. Add garlic, ginger, mushrooms, and stir-fry for 1 minute. Add salt, snow peas, tree ears, pressed bean curd, wine, oyster sauce, sugar, and stock. Cook and stir for about 5 seconds. Stir in the dissolved cornstarch and cook until sauce becomes thick. Serve hot.
Serves 4

MOCK ROAST DUCK

 Mock Roast Duck is not at all hard to make—and you can prepare it a couple days in advance. Leftover Mock Roast Duck is wonderful stir-fried with vegetables such as broccoli, cabbage, cauliflower, bok choy, and even with fried rice.

>   3 Tbsps soy sauce
>   1 tsp sugar
>   1 Tbsp Shao-sing wine, dry sherry, or sake
>   ½ cup mushroom water*
>   5 Tbsps oil
>   10 dried bean curd sheets, about 8 by 14 inches each
>   1 Tbsp sesame oil

* Made by soaking 6 medium-sized dried Chinese mushrooms in ⅔ cup hot water for 1 hour; the mushrooms are removed and the liquid used.

In a small saucepan combine soy sauce, sugar, wine, mushroom water, and sesame oil. Simmer the sauce over a slow flame for 5 minutes and let cool.

Soak bean curd sheets in warm water for 2 minutes and pat dry with paper towels. Spread one sheet on a flat surface and brush soy sauce mixture generously all over the sheet. Spread another sheet on top of the first one; again brush soy sauce mixture over the entire surface of the second sheet. Repeat until all the bean curd sheets are coated with the soy sauce mixture and stacked in one pile. (Save the leftover soy sauce mixture.) Fold three times across the shorter side and cut the folded bean curd strip crosswise in half. Wrap strips securely with gauze.

Place wrapped bean curd strips in a steamer and steam for 15 minutes. Take bean curd strips from steamer and remove the gauze.

Heat oil in a skillet over a moderate flame and fry both sides of bean curd strips in oil until they become golden brown. Drain off excess oil from pan and pour in the remaining soy sauce mixture (add extra stock if needed). Cover pan, and simmer for 5 minutes, then cool.

Cut each strip crosswise into pieces ½ inch wide. Arrange them neatly on a platter and serve.
Serves 4

素油鷄 MOCK SOY SAUCE CHICKEN

The original way of making Mock Chicken was to use only bai-yeh hundred-leaf bean curd sheets. Bai-yeh is made of bean curd, and when there are several layers of them cooked together, they turn soft and tend to stick to each other. Alternating hundred-leaf bean curd sheets with dried bean curd sheets gives the dish a very nice texture, because dried bean curd sheets are made from soy milk and are chewy. Leftover Mock Soy Sauce Chicken is also very good stir-fried with vegetables.

> ¼ tsp baking soda
> 8 sheets fresh or frozen hundred-leaf bean curd
>   sheets 8 by 6 inches
> 4 sheets dried bean curd sheets, 8 by 6 inches
> 3 slices ginger, about 1 inch in diameter
> 3 scallions cut into 1-inch sections
> 1 Tbsp Shao-sing wine, dry sherry, or sake
> 3 Tbsps soy sauce
> 1 tsp sugar
> ½ cup stock
> 1 tsp sesame oil
> 1 Tbsp oil

Dissolve baking soda in 4 cups hot water. Soak hundred-leaf bean curd sheets in the baking soda solution for 5 minutes. Rinse them thoroughly in fresh water 3 to 4 times, and drain.

Soak dried bean curd sheets in warm water for about 2 minutes. Drain.

Spread 1 dried bean curd sheet on a flat surface and place 2 hundred-leaf bean curd sheets on top of it evenly. Spread another sheet of dried bean curd sheet on top of the hundred-leaf and top with 2 more hundred-leaf sheets. Fold the whole thing up into a 2 by 6-inch flat strip. Squeeze out excess water in the strip, or press it with a heavy board for a few minutes. Repeat this procedure with the remaining bean curd sheets. Cut each strip crosswise in half. Wrap strips securely with gauze.

Place bean curd strips in a steamer and steam for 15 minutes. Take bean curd strips from steamer and remove the gauze. Heat oil in a skillet over a moderate fire and brown both sides of the bean curd strips in oil. Add ginger, scallions, wine, soy sauce, sugar, stock, and sesame oil. Mix everything thoroughly, cover, and simmer over a low flame for 5 minutes.

Cut each piece of bean curd strip crosswise into ½-inch pieces. Arrange them neatly on a plate, pour sauce over them, and serve.
Serves 4

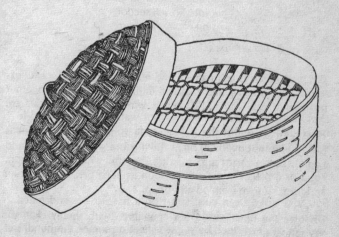

MOCK VELVET CHICKEN

(Fried Bean Curd with Egg Whites)

To the best of my knowledge, this is my exclusive innovation; I wish I could get it patented. It is very elegant.

    2 squares fresh firm bean curd, about 3 by 3 inches
    5 egg whites, slightly beaten
    ½ tsp salt
    ½ Tbsp Shao-sing wine, dry sherry, or sake
    2 tsps cornstarch
    1 cup oil
    1 cup stock
    ½ Tbsp light soy sauce
    ½ tsp sugar
    Dash pepper
    ½ cup frozen peas, defrosted
    1 tsp sesame oil

Wrap the bean curd in gauze and extract the water by squeezing. Put in a bowl and mash it until very fine. Mix together bean curd, egg whites, ¼ tsp salt, wine, and 1 tsp cornstarch.

Heat oil in a small skillet over a medium flame. When the oil is just hot (do not overheat oil as the mixture should stay soft and white), scoop bean curd mixture into oil with a tablespoon. Fry 5 or 6 pieces at a time; as soon as each piece turns white and firm, remove from oil and drain.

Dissolve the remaining 1 tsp cornstarch with the stock, light soy sauce, sugar, the remaining salt, and pepper. Empty all but

1 Tbsp oil in the pan and set it back over a medium flame. Add stock mixture and peas and bring to a boil. Stir and cook until the sauce is thick and smooth, then fold in the fried bean curd and add sesame oil. Transfer to a plate and serve at once.
Serves 4

SPICY MOCK CHICKEN

This is an especially luscious dish. Do try it. The sauce can also be served with Mock Roast Duck and with Mock Ham.

    1 recipe Mock Soy Sauce Chicken (see page 144)
       but use only 1 Tbsp soy sauce
    1 Tbsp finely chopped scallion
    1 tsp minced garlic
    1 tsp minced ginger
    1 Tbsp wine vinegar
    ½ tsp sugar
    2 Tbsps soy sauce
    1 tsp chili oil or Tabasco sauce
    ½ tsp toasted ground Szechuan peppercorn
       powder (see recipe, page 168)
    1 Tbsp sesame oil
    ¼ cup chopped roasted peanuts

Prepare the Mock Soy Sauce Chicken according to the recipe. Arrange the cut-up bean curd strips neatly on a plate, but do not pour the sauce from that recipe over the mock chicken—discard it.

In a small bowl, mix together all the ingredients listed above except the chopped peanuts. Pour the sauce evenly over the mock chicken and sprinkle chopped peanuts on top. Serve cold.
Serves 4

MOCK HAM

7 oz dried bean curd sheets
3 Tbsp oil
5 scallions, washed
5 slices fresh ginger
¼ cup soy sauce
2 tsp sugar
1 cup stock

Soak dried bean curd sheets in warm water for 2 minutes and pat dry with paper towels. Cut bean curd sheets into ¼-inch strips.

Set a saucepan over a moderate flame and add oil. Drop in scallions and ginger slices and brown them in hot oil for 1 minute. Add soy sauce, sugar, and stock, simmer over low flame for 5 minutes.

Remove scallions and ginger from sauce. Mix bean curd strips with the sauce and let them marinate for 15 minutes. Drain off sauce.

Spread gauze on a flat surface. Pile bean curd strips on top of the gauze and roll the bean curd up tightly into a big roll about 2 inches in diameter. Wrap in gauze and tie securely with string. Place the tied-up bean curd roll in a steamer and steam for 1 hour.

Remove bean curd roll from steamer and let cool. Cut away string and unwrap gauze. Slice the role crosswise into pieces about ⅛-inch thick, arrange on plate, and serve.
Serves 4

MOCK ABALONE
(Braised Gluten Balls)

10 dried Chinese mushrooms, about 2 inches
   in diameter each
8 oz fried gluten balls, commercial or homemade
   (see recipe, page 166)
2 Tbsps soy sauce
1 Tbsp Shao-sing wine, dry sherry, or sake
1 tsp minced ginger
1 cup mushroom water (cooking liquid from the dried
   Chinese mushrooms)
1 tsp sugar
½ cup sliced bamboo shoots
½ Tbsp sesame oil

Wash mushrooms and soak them in 1 cup hot water for 30 minutes. Drain, reserving the liquid. Cut off stems from mushrooms and then cut caps in halves. Simmer mushrooms in same liquid in saucepan over low flame for 20 minutes.

Place fried gluten balls in a wok or a saucepan and add cooked mushrooms and juice, soy sauce, wine, ginger, sugar, and bamboo shoots. Mix ingredients thoroughly, cover, and simmer over a low flame for 30 minutes.

Uncover, add sesame oil, and transfer contents to a serving plate. Serve hot, or cold if dish is prepared in advance.
Serves 4

MOCK MU-SHU PORK

素
木
須
肉

Mu-Shu Pork has become almost as popular as Sweet and Sour Pork in the United States. In this recipe the pork has been replaced with five-spice pressed bean curd. Traditionally this dish is served with *bao-bing*, a crepe-like pancake—in this book called Mandarin Tortillas; one eats it by putting about 3 tablespoonsful of Mu-Shu "Pork" on the *bao-bing*, and then rolling the whole thing up like an enchilada and eating it with the hands. If you do not have the time to prepare the Mandarin Tortillas, this dish goes perfectly well with rice.

- ½ cup soaked tiger lily buds
- 1 cup soaked tree ears
- 3 Tbsps oil
- 3 eggs, lightly beaten
- ½ cup shredded scallion
- 2 squares five-spice pressed bean curd, shredded (see recipe, page 123)
- ½ cup shredded bamboo shoots
- 1 cup soaked mung bean noodles cut in 2-inch lengths
- 2 Tbsps soy sauce
- 1 Tbsp Shao-sing wine, dry sherry, or sake
- ½ tsp sugar
- ¼ tsp salt
- ¼ cup stock
- 1 recipe Mandarin Tortillas (see page 241)

Prepare Mandarin Tortillas according to recipe.

Prepare tree ears and tiger lily buds as instructed on page 167.

Set wok or skillet over high flame and add ½ Tbsp oil. Pour in the beaten eggs, swirl around, and cook until the eggs are set.

Remove eggs to plate and break them into small pieces with a fork or a knife.

Set the wok or skillet back over a high flame and pour in the remaining oil. When oil is very hot, add scallion and pressed bean curd and cook for 30 seconds. Then add bamboo shoots, tiger lily buds, tree ears, and mung bean noodles, and stir all the ingredients thoroughly. Add soy sauce, wine, sugar, salt, and stock; cook over moderate flame until liquid evaporates, and then add eggs. Mix well with the rest of the contents of the pan. Transfer Mu-Shu Pork to a plate and serve with Mandarin Tortillas.
Serves 4

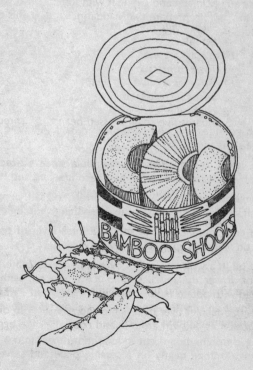

MOCK SHRIMP TOAST

Shrimp toast is considered an elegant dish and is usually served as one of the hors d'oeuvres at the beginning of a formal dinner. Real shrimp toast is made with ground fresh shrimp mixed with chopped pork fat, egg, and seasonings.

½ lb potatoes
1 small carrot
4 slices white bread, toasted
1 tsp salt
Dash black pepper
1 Tbsp cornstarch
1 tsp sesame oil
2 Tbsps sesame seed
2 cups oil

Wash potatoes and boil until they are soft. Allow to cool. Remove skins and mash.

Peel carrot and cut into chunks. In a small saucepan cover carrot with water and boil until it becomes soft, and then mash.

Mix mashed potato with mashed carrot. Add salt, pepper, cornstarch, and sesame oil and mix everything thoroughly.

Trim crust from toast and spread a thick layer of potato mixture on one side. Sprinkle with sesame seed.

Heat oil in a wok or a skillet over a moderate flame. When oil is hot, lower the mock shrimp toast into oil, with the side spread with potato mixture down. Fry for about 2 minutes, and turn over and fry the other side for about 15 seconds. Repeat with remaining pieces of toast.

On a chopping board cut mock shrimp toast into 1 by 2-inch pieces. Arrange neatly on a serving plate and serve at once.

Serves 4

MOCK SHANGHAI EELS

Real eels and imitation eels made with mushrooms are both considered delicacies by the Chinese. Thus, this is a special treat dish for guests.

1½ oz dried Chinese mushrooms
2 Tbsps flour
1 tsp minced garlic
1 cup oil
½ cup shredded bamboo shoots or 1 cup bean sprouts
1 Tbsp oyster sauce
1 Tbsp soy sauce
1 tsp sugar
⅓ cup stock or liquid from cooking the mushrooms
1 tsp sesame oil

Wash mushrooms and soak them in 2 cups of hot water for 30 minutes. Drain mushrooms, pouring the soaking water into a saucepan. Remove stems from mushrooms and cut into thin strips. Drop mushroom strips into the saucepan with soaking water and simmer over a low flame for 20 minutes. Drain, and reserve the liquid. Mix mushrooms with flour.

Heat oil in a wok. When oil is hot, fry mushrooms for about 10 seconds. Remove from oil and drain.

Drain all but 1 Tbsp oil from wok. Reheat, and add garlic, bamboo shoots or bean sprouts, oyster sauce, soy sauce, sugar, and stock (or mushroom liquid). Bring to a boil, then add mushrooms, stir, and cook for 1 minute, and serve hot.
Serves 4

炒 FRIED MOCK
假 SQUAB
白
鴿
鬆
松

Despite the long list of ingredients, this delicious dish
is not difficult to make. It can be prepared in advance
and reheated.

- ½ cup soaked and chopped tree ears
- 2 Tbsps oil
- 1 tsp minced ginger
- 1 cup chopped water chestnuts
- 1 cup chopped canned mushrooms
- 1 cup chopped pressed bean curd (see recipe, page 122), or five-spice pressed bean curd (see recipe, page 123)
- 2 Tbsps oyster sauce
- 1 Tbsp soy sauce
- 1 tsp Shao-sing wine, dry sherry, or sake
- ½ tsp sugar
- ½ cup stock
- ½ cup defrosted frozen peas
- ½ Tbsp cornstarch dissolved in 2 Tbsps water
- 20 pieces leaf lettuce or Boston lettuce, each about 5 inches across

Prepare tree ears according to instructions on page 167.

Set a wok or skillet over a high flame, add oil and ginger, and
cook for 5 seconds. Add water chestnuts, mushrooms, tree ears,
and pressed bean curd, stir, and cook for 1 minute. Add oyster
sauce, soy sauce, wine, sugar, stock, and mix thoroughly. Stir
and cook everything for 1 more minute. Thicken with dissolved
cornstarch. Transfer to a serving plate and serve on lettuce
leaves.
Serves 4

MOCK SWEET AND SOUR PORK

素
咕
嚕
肉

3 cups oil
1 medium sized green pepper, seeded and cut into 1-inch squares
1 cup shelled walnuts, each walnut halved
¼ cup cornstarch
¼ cup flour
1 Tbsp soy sauce
1 medium carrot, cut into small wedges, boiled in water for 5 minutes and drained
1 small can sliced pineapple, cut into small chunks

For the sauce
2 Tbsps sugar
¼ cup crabapple sauce or catsup
¼ cup vinegar
1 Tbsp soy sauce
½ cup unsweetened pineapple juice from canned pineapple
1 tsp minced garlic
1 Tbsp cornstarch dissolved in 2 Tbsps water

In a bowl for the sauce combine sugar, crabapple sauce, vinegar, soy sauce, and pineapple juice; stir well, and set aside.

Set a wok or a skillet over a moderate flame, add 1 Tbsp oil, and add the green pepper. Stir-fry for 1 minute, then transfer to a plate.

Heat 1 Tbsp oil in a saucepan. When oil is hot, add garlic, and then the sweet and sour sauce. Bring to a boil, stir, and cook until sugar dissolves. Thicken sauce with dissolved cornstarch. Remove from flame, but keep warm.

Heat remaining oil in a wok or a deep-frier over a moderate flame. Wipe walnuts with a piece of damp cloth or paper towel and remove the crumbs. Drop walnuts in oil and deep-fry until they become light brown. Scoop walnuts from oil and cool on a piece of paper towel, leaving oil in wok.

In a bowl mix cornstarch, flour, soy sauce, and ¼ cup water to form a smooth batter. Drop walnuts into mixture and stir until each piece of walnut is coated with batter. Deep-fry them once more in hot oil until golden brown. Remove the walnuts from oil and drain.

Mix fried walnuts with the sweet and sour sauce and pepper, carrot, and pineapple. Serve at once.
Serves 4

素麵鍋肉 MOCK TWICE-COOKED PORK

Twice-cooked pork is one of the best-known Szechuan dishes. In the meat version, the pork is first boiled, then cut into paper-thin slices and added to the sauce at the same time the pressed bean curd goes in. The vegetarian version is as follows.

    2 squares five-spice pressed bean curd (see recipe,
      page 123)
    1 large leek or 5 scallions
    2 medium-sized green peppers
    4 Tbsps oil
    1 tsp minced garlic
    1 Tbsp sweet bean paste
    1 Tbsp Szechuan hot bean paste

1 Tbsp soy sauce
1 tsp sugar
1 Tbsp Shao-sing wine, dry sherry, or sake
¼ cup stock

Slice five-spice pressed bean curd into 1-inch by 1½-inch pieces.

Wash leek thoroughly, then roll-cut diagonally into 1½-inch pieces.

Seed and de-rib green peppers. Cut into wedges about the same size as the pressed bean curd.

Set a wok or skillet over a high flame, add 2 Tbsps oil, and drop in green peppers. Stir and toss for 1 minute; add leek and stir-fry both ingredients for 1 more minute; remove to a dish.

Heat the remaining oil. Stir in garlic, and cook for 15 seconds. Add sweet bean paste, hot bean paste, soy sauce, sugar, and pressed bean curd. Toss and blend the ingredients for 1 minute. Add green peppers and leek, wine, and stock and mix everything thoroughly. Transfer to plate and serve.
Serves 4

素
蝦
丸

MOCK SHRIMP BALLS

The sweet and sour sauce for Mock Sweet and Sour Pork can be used to make sweet and sour shrimp balls as well.

½ lb potatoes
½ cup finely shredded carrot
⅓ cup finely shredded icicle radish or white
   Chinese radish
1 egg, beaten
2 Tbsps Shao-sing wine, dry sherry, or sake
1 tsp salt
Dash white pepper
2 Tbsps chopped scallion
3 Tbsps cornstarch or 1½ Tbsps cornstarch and 1½
   Tbsps rice powder
2 cups oil
Toasted Szechuan peppercorn salt (see recipe,
   page 168) or chili pepper paste for dipping

Wash potatoes and boil until they are soft. Allow to cook. Remove the skins and mash.

In a bowl mix mashed potatoes with shredded carrot, shredded radish, egg, wine, salt, pepper, scallion, and cornstarch. Beat with a fork until everything is well blended.

Heat oil in a wok or a deep fryer over a moderate flame. When oil is hot, with your hand and a teaspoon scoop up marble-sized balls of potato mixture and deep-fry 8 to 10 balls at a time. When balls turn golden color, remove them from oil and drain. Repeat until all the mixture is used. Serve hot with Szechuan peppercorn salt or with chili pepper paste.
Serves 4

BEAN CURD WITH THOUSAND-YEAR EGGS

豆
腐
妙
皮
蛋

A dish full of yin and yang contrasts: white and black, soft and crunchy, and as easy as ABC.

2 thousand-year eggs
3 squares fresh bean curd
½ tsp minced ginger
1 Tbsp chopped scallion
2 Tbsps oil
¼ tsp salt
1 Tbsp soy sauce
Dash black pepper
½ cup stock
1 tsp cornstarch dissolved in Tbsp water
1 tsp sesame oil
1 Tbsp chopped fresh coriander (optional)

Scrape the mud from the thousand-year eggs and rinse under running water until all the mud is removed. Tap each one against the table and remove the shell. Dice the eggs into ½-inch pieces.

Rinse bean curd and cut into 1-inch squares about ½ inch thick.

Heat oil in a wok or a skillet, stir in ginger and scallion, and cook for 10 seconds. Add bean curd, salt, soy sauce, pepper, and stock, and bring everything to a boil. Stir in cornstarch and, when sauce thickens, add thousand-year eggs and sesame oil. Transfer contents to serving bowl and sprinkle coriander on top if desired. Serve hot or at room temperature.

Serves 4

VEGETABLE DISHES
AND EGG DISHES

Stop saying that a vegetarian diet
is not diverse enough. One must
realize that beans and corn contain
the true flavor of food.

—*Family Teaching of the Yen Clan*

HOW TO GROW BEAN SPROUTS

Mung bean sprouts are widely available in Oriental grocery stores and supermarkets. In case you have trouble getting them, here are instructions for sprouting them at home.

In order to obtain plump, juicy, crunchy, and tasty bean sprouts, the beans must be from a comparatively recent crop and of high quality. The beans you have had on the kitchen shelves on display for a long time will very likely not give a satisfactory crop. Even those from the store are not always very new. So don't be too disappointed if you don't always get good results. Just keep trying.

Wash ½ to 1 cup mung beans in water thoroughly; put beans in lukewarm water and soak overnight or for at least 14 hours. Soak a large clean clay flowerpot in water until completely saturated. Or take a large metal or styrofoam container and punch 8 to 10 holes in the bottom. Wet a piece of gauze and fold into 4 layers, placing it on the bottom of the pot. Spread beans evenly over the gauze, cover with a wet dish towel, and set a light weight over them. The weight should not be too heavy—just enough to give a little downward push to prevent the beans from shooting upward too quickly and becoming slim instead of plump. The weight used can be a plate or a pie pan that will fit inside the container and cover the entire surface of the beans. Cover the pot tightly with a lid or a board. If you have a dark kitchen you can just set the whole thing on top of the drainboard for easy watering; otherwise, place it in a dark corner or under the sink. Once in the morning, once at noon, and once at night, gently run tepid water over the beans without lifting the gauze or disturbing the beans. Be sure the beans are well saturated.

The beans should be fully mature in 5 days, but this will vary, depending on the temperature in the room. When sprouts are ready for eating, the white part between the head and the root tail should be about 1½ inches long. The whole length of the sprout including the tail stretches to 2½ inches. Don't mistake the tail (which comes out first) for the main body.

Fill the sink with water. Drop in 4 or 5 cups of bean sprouts, then with the hand or a large spoon agitate sprouts briskly to separate the bean husks from the sprouts. The empty husks will float to the top. With a strainer, scoop up the husks and discard them. Remove clean sprouts and drain. Repeat until all the bean sprouts are clean. If they are not to be used immediately, store sprouts in plastic bags and keep in the refrigerator.

麵 **WHEAT GLUTEN**

筋 *(Mein Jin or Vegetable Steak)*

Wheat gluten is one of the essential ingredients in Chinese Buddhist cooking. It is used extensively in many of the mock meat dishes. This rubbery substance is made by removing the starch element from regular wheat flour by rinsing a piece of dough with water until the starch is completely washed out. Gluten has very high nutritive value.

Wheat gluten comes in several forms. Fried, dried, steamed, boiled, canned, and frozen gluten are available at Chinese grocery stores, or can be made at home according to the recipes given in this book. Both fried and steamed gluten will keep indefinitely when frozen. Steamed and boiled gluten have a somewhat chewy texture and are used for making dishes such as mock roast pork. Fried gluten usually comes in the shape of a golf ball and is golden brown in color. When cooked with a sauce it turns soft, slippery, and is very delicious, as it absorbs any flavor that goes in the same dish. If you can knead dough, making wheat gluten will not be a challenge.

> 2 tsps salt
> 2 cups water
> 6 cups flour

Dissolve the salt in water. Mix the salted water with flour to form a soft dough. Knead the dough for about 5 minutes, or until it becomes smooth. Cover dough with a damp cloth or a piece of plastic and let it set for 3 hours or longer.

Fill a large basin or a sink with water. Submerge the dough in water and knead until water becomes milky white. Pour out milky water from the basin and replenish with fresh water and knead dough again in the clear water. Repeat this process until the water no longer turns milky. The remaining dough is wheat gluten.

Both fried gluten and boiled gluten can be kept in the freezer for an indefinite time.

FRIED GLUTEN BALLS

Heat 3 cups oil in a wok over a moderate flame. Cut gluten into small pieces, each piece about the size of a marble. Dry them thoroughly with paper towels; then drop 5 pieces at a time into the hot oil and fry until they puff up 2 or 3 times their original size and become golden brown. Remove from oil and drain.

BOILED GLUTEN

Place the whole piece of gluten (or cut up into 2 or 3 pieces) in a saucepan and cover with water. Boil gluten over a low flame for 20 minutes. Remove from water and drain.

HOW TO PREPARE DRIED INGRIEDENTS

Agar Agar Threads (for salad)
Cut in 2-inch sections, soak in cold water for 30 minutes, rinse with clear water, and drain.

Mushrooms, Dried Chinese

Rinse mushrooms in warm water, then soak them in hot water for 30 minutes. Drain. Remove tough stems.

Mushrooms, Dried Straw

Rinse dried straw mushrooms, then soak in warm water for 15 minutes.

Noodles, Mung Bean

Pour hot water over noodles, soak for 30 minutes, and drain.

Tiger Lily Buds

Place tiger lily buds in a bowl, cover with hot water and soak for 15 minutes, then rinse with clear water. Cut off tough stem ends, then cut each bud in half crosswise.

Tree Ears

Place tree ears in a bowl, pour boiling water over them, and soak for 30 minutes. Rinse thoroughly with clean water to remove sand and cut off the woody part of the bottom.

Seaweed, Hair

Soak hair seaweed in hot water for at least 1 hour. Wash in 2 cups of warm water mixed with 1 Tbsp oil, then rinse with warm water until it runs clear. Drain, and squeeze out excess water.

SZECHUAN PEPPERCORN SALT

3 Tbsps salt
2 Tbsps Szechuan peppercorns

Combine salt and Szechuan peppercorns in an unoiled cast-iron skillet and toast them over a low flame for about 5 minutes. Remove from fire and cool. Grind with mortar and pestle, then sift with a fine strainer. Use the powder which comes out of the strainer and discard the parts remaining in the strainer.

SZECHUAN PEPPERCORN POWDER

3 Tbsps Szechuan peppercorns

Over a low flame, toast Szechuan peppercorns in an unoiled cast-iron skillet for about 5 minutes. Grind with mortar and pestle, then sift with a fine strainer. Save the powder which comes out of the strainer and discard the parts remaining in the strainer.

LO HAN VEGETABLE DISH

This is a deluxe and classic version of this renowned dish. A simpler version may be prepared by using just 4 or 5 different kinds of ingredients or by omitting vegetable ingredients that are hard to find or do not appeal to you. Though there are no fixed rules for adding ingredients, the dish will not be as interesting and diverse in texture if you use vegetables that belong to the same family. The dish should consist of one type of mushroom, one type of hard vegetable (broccoli, carrot, or cauliflower), and perhaps another vegetable which is semi-hard (bamboo shoots, snow peas, celery, or green pepper), along with something that adds volume to the dish, such as bean sprouts or shredded cabbage. One should also remember to keep the dish rich in texture and color. There should be something crunchy to contrast with something soft, and a quiet color to set off the bright.

   6 medium-sized dried Chinese mushrooms, soaked
   ½ cup soaked tree ears
   ¼ cup dried hair seaweed (optional)
   3 Tbsps oil
   2 slices ginger
   1 Tbsp Shao-sing wine, dry sherry, or sake
   ½ cup canned or 1 cup fresh straw mushrooms
   ½ cup canned or 1 cup fresh button mushrooms
   2 cups celery cabbage or bok choy, or 20 snow peas
   1 cup fresh bean sprouts
   ¼ tsp salt
  10 fried wheat gluten balls (see recipe, page 166)
   ½ cup sliced tender bamboo shoots
  10 baby corn on the cob (optional)
  20 canned gingko nuts
   1 tsp minced ginger

1 Tbsp soy sauce
2 Tbsps oyster sauce
¼ tsp sugar
½ cup stock
1 Tbsp cornstarch dissolved in 2 Tbsps water

Prepare mushrooms and tree ears according to instructions on page 167.

Pour boiling water over hair seaweed, if desired, and allow to stand for 1 hour. Rinse hair seaweed with warm water. Heat a saucepan with ½ Tbsp oil, add fresh ginger, 1 tsp wine, ½ cup water, and hair seaweed. Simmer over a low flame for 5 minutes.

Trim the stems from the dried Chinese black mushrooms and cut each mushroom cap in half. If the straw mushrooms and button mushrooms are very large, cut them in half. In a saucepan cover the dried mushrooms with water, set over a low flame and simmer for 20 minutes.

Heat 1 Tbsp oil in a wok or skillet over high heat. Add celery cabbage (or snow peas or bok choy), bean sprouts, and salt; stir-fry about 30 seconds. Transfer vegetables to a plate and keep warm.

Heat the remaining oil in a wok or a skillet over high heat, then add gluten balls, bamboo shoots, the three kinds of mushrooms, tree ears, hair seaweed, baby corn, gingko nuts, the remaining wine, minced ginger, soy sauce, oyster sauce, sugar, and stock. Mix all the ingredients thoroughly. Cover pan, lower flame, and let cook for about 3 minutes. Uncover pan, thicken sauce with cornstarch, then add the cooked vegetables and blend well. Empty the entire contents on a serving plate and serve hot.
Serves 4 to 6

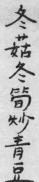

STRING BEANS STIR-FRIED WITH BAMBOO SHOOTS AND MUSHROOMS

This is an unusual way of preparing green beans. Deep-frying dehydrates the beans slightly and gives them a rich flavor. (The beans can be steamed instead of deep-fried, but the taste will not be the same.) This dish can be served hot or cold.

10 dried Chinese mushrooms, about 2 inches
    in diameter
 1 lb string beans
 2 cups oil
 2 Tbsps soy sauce
½ cup sliced bamboo shoots
½ tsp sugar
¼ tsp salt
¼ cup stock

Rinse mushrooms and soak them in 1 cup hot water for 30 minutes. Drain, saving soaking water. Cut each mushroom into 3 sections, removing tough stem. Pour mushrooms and the water into a small saucepan, cover pan, and simmer for 30 minutes over a low flame.

Wash beans in cold water and dry with paper towels. Snap off the tips and remove the strings from both sides. Break beans into 2-inch pieces.

Set a wok over high flame, pour in 2 cups oil, and let heat. Drop in beans and deep-fry for 3 or 4 minutes. Remove beans from oil and drain in a strainer.

In a clean wok or skillet add 1 Tbsp oil from the remaining oil after cooking string beans and set on top of a moderate flame. Add fried beans and cooked mushrooms to pan, add soy sauce, bamboo shoots, sugar, salt, and stock, and cook everything for 2 minutes. Remove beans, mushrooms, and bamboo shoots to a plate and serve.

Serves 4

乾 STRING BEANS
煸 SZECHUAN STYLE
四
季
豆

1 oz Szechuan preserved vegetables
1 lb string beans
2 cups oil
½ Tbsp minced ginger
2 Tbsps chopped scallion
½ tsp salt
1 tsp sugar
1 Tbsp vinegar
1 Tbsp soy sauce
3 Tbsps stock
1 tsp sesame oil

Rinse Szechuan preserved vegetables and chop into small pieces.

Wash beans in cold water and dry with paper towels. Snap off the tips and remove the strings from both sides. Break beans into 2-inch pieces.

Set a wok over high flame, pour in oil, and let heat. Drop in beans and deep-fry for 3 to 4 minutes. Remove beans from oil and drain in a strainer.

Empty all but 2 Tbsps oil from wok and set the wok over a moderate flame. Add ginger, scallion, and Szechuan preserved

vegetables and cook for 30 seconds. Drop in fried beans, add salt, vinegar, soy sauce, and stock, and cook and stir until most of the liquid is evaporated. Mix in sesame oil. Transfer everything to a plate and serve.
Serves 4

豆豉芥菜 CHINESE MUSTARD GREENS IN BLACK BEAN SAUCE

Chinese mustard greens come in two different varieties. The kind for sale at supermarkets usually has a very large head of dark green ruffled leaves with thick stems. The other kind is lighter in color with narrow stems and is available in Chinatown. Both kinds of Chinese mustard greens have a slightly bitter flavor but leave a wonderful after-taste in the mouth. Substitute 1 pound of Chinese radish for Chinese mustard greens and you have another delightful dish with black bean sauce. Peel the radish and cut into 1-inch wedges to prepare for cooking.

　　1 lb thick stem mustard greens
　　1 Tbsp fermented black beans
　　2 Tbsps oil
　　1 tsp minced garlic
　　½ Tbsp Shao-sing wine, dry sherry, or sake
　　1 Tbsp oyster sauce
　　½ tsp sugar
　　¼ tsp salt
　　⅓ cup stock
　　1 tsp cornstarch dissolved in 1 Tbsp water

Separate mustard greens, rinse thoroughly and drain. Cut into 2-inch squares.

Remove grit and other particles from black beans and rinse with water. Mash the beans with mortar and pestle, or put the beans in a small bowl and pound them with the handle of a cleaver.

Heat oil in a wok over a moderate flame. When oil is hot, add black beans and garlic and stir in oil for a few seconds. Drop in mustard greens and stir-fry for 30 seconds. Add wine, oyster sauce, sugar, salt, and stock; mix the ingredients thoroughly, cover wok and cook for 3 minutes. Uncover and stir in dissolved cornstarch. When sauce becomes thick, transfer vegetables to a plate and serve hot.

Serves 4

BRAISED EGGPLANT

Those who are not too crazy about eggplant will have their attitude changed by this dish, because eggplant prepared this way tastes like mushrooms.

- 1 lb eggplant
- 2 oz Szechuan preserved vegetable
- 4 Tbsps oil
- 4 cloves garlic, peeled and crushed
- 1 tsp minced ginger
- 1 Tbsp soy sauce
- ½ Tbsp Shao-sing wine, or dry sherry, or sake
- 1 tsp sugar
- ½ cup stock

Wash eggplant and dry with paper towels. (If very large eggplant are used, peel off the skins.) Cut eggplant lengthwise into 1-inch strips, then cut the strips crosswise into 2-inch long pieces.

Rinse Szechuan preserved vegetable and then chop into fine pieces. Set aside.

Set a wok over high flame; when wok is hot, add oil and then garlic and cook garlic in oil for a few seconds. Add ginger and eggplant and stir-fry over a moderate flame for 1 minute. Add chopped Szechuan preserved vegetable, soy sauce, wine, sugar, and stock; cover wok and simmer over a low flame for 5 minutes, or until eggplant is tender and the sauce has been absorbed. If the eggplant is done and there is still plenty of liquid left, turn the flame up to high and boil the sauce rapidly until it evaporates. Transfer eggplant to a plate and serve hot or cold.
Serves 4

FINE JADE MEETS THREE NUNS

(Asparagus with Three Kinds of Mushrooms)

In Chinese the word for "mushrooms" and the word for "nuns" sound exactly alike. The asparagus is the jade, and the character for "meet" sounds like the character for the cooking term "to blend"—hence the green jade is meeting with three nuns.

If using three kinds of mushrooms is too expensive, you can cut down to two kinds or one kind (and of course change the name of the dish slightly). When asparagus is not in season, use fresh broccoli.

> 10 dried Chinese mushrooms, about 1-inch in diameter (if larger ones are used, cut them in half.)
> ½ cup fresh or canned straw mushrooms
> ½ cup canned button mushrooms
> 12 stalks fresh asparagus
> 3 Tbsps oil
> 1 Tbsp oyster sauce
> 1 Tbsp soy sauce
> ¼ tsp sugar
> ½ tsp salt
> ¼ cup stock
> ½ Tbsp cornstarch dissolved in 1 Tbsp water
> 1 tsp sesame oil

Rinse dried Chinese mushrooms and soak them in hot water for 30 minutes. Drain and remove tough stems. In a small saucepan cover mushrooms with water and simmer over a low flame for 30 minutes.

Rinse straw mushrooms and button mushrooms and drain.

Snap off the tough end of each stalk of asparagus. Rinse stalks well and drain. Cut each stalk diagonally into 1-inch pieces. In a saucepan cover asparagus with 2 cups water. Bring to a boil, then simmer uncovered for 2 minutes, or until asparagus is just cooked. Drain off the liquid.

Set a wok or skillet over a medium flame and add 1 Tbsp oil. When the oil is hot, drop in the cooked asparagus and gently stir-fry for a few seconds. Remove to a warm plate and keep warm.

Set a clean wok over a medium flame and add the remaining oil. When oil is hot, add oyster sauce, soy sauce, sugar, salt, stock, and then the three kinds of mushrooms. Cook mushrooms in sauce for a few seconds, and then thicken sauce with dissolved cornstarch. Combine the asparagus with the mushrooms and add sesame oil. Transfer to a plate and serve at once Serves 4

SPICY EGGPLANT

This is a Szechuan dish, so add as much chili pepper paste as you can take. This very rich and delicious dish can be served hot or cold.

    1 lb eggplant
    2 cups oil
    ½ Tbsp minced garlic
    1 Tbsp minced ginger
    ½ Tbsp Shao-sing wine, dry sherry, or sake
    1 Tbsp hot bean paste
    ½ Tbsp chili pepper paste
    1 Tbsp soy sauce
    ½ tsp sugar
    1 Tbsp vinegar
    2 Tbsps chopped scallion
    ½ cup stock
    1 tsp cornstarch dissolved in 1 Tbsp water
    1 tsp sesame oil

Peel eggplant and cut into ¾ by ¾ by 4-inch strips.

Heat oil in a wok or a deep fryer until very hot. Deep-fry eggplant strips in hot oil for about 1 minute or until the strips become soft. Remove eggplant from oil and drain in a strainer.

Set a wok or skillet over a high flame. Pour in 2 Tbsps oil; when oil is hot, add garlic and ginger and stir-fry for 1 minute. Add eggplant, wine, hot bean paste, chili pepper paste, soy sauce, sugar, vinegar, chopped scallion, and stock. Blend everything thoroughly and cook for 2 minutes. Add dissolved cornstarch and cook until sauce becomes thick. Add sesame oil; transfer to plate and serve.
Serves 4

乾
燒
黃
瓜

STIR-FRIED CUCUMBER

For people who are used to eating cucumbers raw, this recipe may sound a bit strange. But it is very Chinese to cook cucumbers. This dish is so delicious that one of my students cooked it every day for two weeks. It is spicy and hot on the outside yet crunchy and soothing in the center. Zucchini can be cooked the same way, but the skin should be left on.

     2 large cucumbers or 3 small ones
     1 Tbsp oil
     ½ Tbsp minced garlic
     1 tsp minced ginger
     ½ Tbsp chopped fresh chili pepper or
       ½ Tbsp chili paste
     1 Tbsp soy sauce
     ¼ tsp sugar
     ¼ tsp salt

Peel cucumbers and cut each one in half lengthwise, and then remove the seeds. Cut each half in two lengthwise again and cut each section crosswise into 1½-inch pieces.

Set a wok or a skillet over a high flame and add oil. When oil is hot, drop in garlic, ginger, and chili pepper or paste, and stir ingredients for a few seconds. Add cucumber and stir-fry for 1 minute. Add soy sauce, sugar, and salt, and stir and cook until cucumber becomes soft. Remove cucumber to a plate and serve hot.
Serves 4

炒 STIR-FRIED
白 BOK CHOY

菜　This is a basic stir-frying method for high water-content vegetables. The bok choy can be replaced with Swiss chard, Chinese celery cabbage, regular cabbage, zucchini, and other high-moisture vegetables.

> 1 lb bok choy
> 2 Tbsps oil
> 1 tsp minced garlic or minced ginger
> ½ tsp salt
> ¼ tsp sugar
> ½ Tbsp Shao-sing wine, dry sherry, or sake
> 1 tsp fish or 1 Tbsp oyster sauce
> ¼ cup stock
> ½ tsp cornstarch dissolved in ½ Tbsp water

Separate bok choy stalks and rinse thoroughly, trimming off withered leaves. Cut the stalks diagonally into 2-inch lengths.

Heat oil in a wok or a skillet over a high flame, stir in garlic or ginger, and cook for 10 seconds. Add salt, then bok choy and toss and turn for 1 minute to coat the vegetable with oil. Add sugar, wine, fish sauce, and stock; cover and cook for 1 minute. Uncover and stir in the dissolved cornstarch, mix well, and transfer to plate and serve at once.

Serves 4

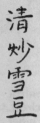

STIR-FRIED SNOW PEAS

12 oz fresh snow peas
 2 Tbsps oil
 1 tsp salt
10 water chestnuts, sliced
 1 tsp Shao-sing wine, dry sherry, or sake
¼ tsp sugar
 3 Tbsps stock

Snap off both tips of snow peas and remove strings from the sides. Wash peas in cold water and shake off excess water.

Set wok or skillet over high flame and pour in oil. When oil is hot, add salt and then the peas and water chestnuts. Stir pea pods constantly for 1 minute to prevent burning. Add wine, sugar, and stock. Lower flame to medium, and stir-fry for about 1 minute. Transfer snow peas and water chestnuts to a plate and serve at once.
Serves 4

STIR-FRIED GREEN BEANS

For a variation of this dish, replace green beans with 12 oz cabbage. Cut cabbage into 1-inch lengths or shred coarsely, and use only ⅓ cup stock.

    1 lb tender green beans
    2 Tbsps oil
    2 large cloves garlic, crushed or minced
    ½ tsp salt
    ⅔ cup stock or water

Wash beans in cold water and dry with paper towels. Snap off the tips and remove the strings from both sides. Break beans or cut them diagonally into 2-inch pieces.

Heat oil in a wok over a high flame. Drop in garlic and stir for a few seconds; then add salt and beans and toss and stir beans for 1 minute. Add stock, cover pan, and cook for about 4 minutes. Uncover, stir the beans again, and cook until most of the liquid is evaporated. Transfer to plate and serve hot.
Serves 4

STIR-FRIED BROCCOLI

This simple way of cooking broccoli is most delicious. It can be served as an all-purpose vegetable with a Chinese or a Western meal.

Cauliflower can be cooked the same way. Break the flowery part into small pieces; split thick stems in half and cut them diagonally into 1-inch pieces.

> 1 lb fresh broccoli
> 2 Tbsps oil
> ½ tsp salt
> ½ Tbsp Shao-sing wine, dry sherry, or sake
> ½ cup stock or water

Wash broccoli and shake off the water, stalk by stalk. With a small knife peel off the tough skin from the stems by inserting the knife between the skin and the soft part of the stem at the tip of the stalk and pulling toward the flowery part. Cut the flowerets into pieces 2 inches long by ⅔-inch in diameter. Slice the stems diagonally into 2 by ½-inch pieces.

Set a wok over a high flame and pour in oil. When oil is hot, add salt and then broccoli, and stir the vegetables around for 1 minute. Add stock, cover pan and cook for 2 to 3 minutes over high flame. Remove lid, scoop broccoli onto a plate, and serve at once.

Serves 4

炒 STIR-FRIED SPINACH

菜 菠

To give this dish an authentic taste, freshly picked spinach is recommended. In China, spinach is sold in clumps with the sweet pinkish roots still attached to the leaves; the roots are cut up and cooked with the leaves. Occasionally, in supermarkets and often in Chinatown markets, spinach can be bought with the roots uncut. For variation, substitute beet greens for spinach.

        1½ lbs fresh spinach
         3 Tbsps oil
         1 tsp minced garlic
        ½ tsp salt
         1 Tbsp Shao-sing wine, dry sherry, or sake
        ½ tsp sugar
         1 tsp fish sauce
        ½ tsp cornstarch dissolved in 1 Tbsp water
         1 tsp sesame oil

Wash spinach with several changes of water. Cut into pieces 2 inches long; if you do find the vegetable with the roots still attached, first cut each root lengthwise in half (or cut the thicker ones into quarters), then cut crosswise into small sections.

Heat oil in a wok over high flame, stir in garlic and salt, and cook for 10 seconds. Then drop in spinach and toss and turn constantly for 2 minutes. Add wine, sugar, and fish sauce, blend, and cook for 1 more minute. Thicken the juice with dissolved cornstarch and then stir in sesame oil. Transfer to a plate and serve at once.
Serves 4

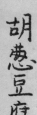

STIR-FRIED LEEKS WITH BEAN CURD

The delicate taste of the leeks and velvety texture of the bean curd make a perfect combination. This dish is very easy to prepare and incredibly good.

½ lb leeks
2 Tbsps oil
3 squares soft fresh bean curd
½ tsp salt
¼ tsp sugar
1 Tbsp soy sauce
¼ cup stock
1 tsp cornstarch dissolved in 1 Tbsp water
Dash black pepper

Wash leeks thoroughly, then roll-cut diagonally into pieces 1 inch long. Cut bean curd into 1-inch squares.

Heat oil in a wok or a skillet over a high flame. Drop in leeks and stir-fry until they become soft and even slightly burned. Add bean curd, salt, sugar, soy sauce, and stock, bring to a boil, and then simmer for 2 minutes. Thicken with dissolved cornstarch and sprinkle with black pepper. Serve hot.
Serves 4

毛豆炒麻菇 FRESH SOYBEANS STIR-FRIED WITH FRESH MUSHROOMS

This is a seasonal dish—the soybeans must be freshly picked. Substitute fresh lima beans if soybeans are not available. For variation, substitute 2 cups shredded green pepper.

⅔ cup fresh shelled soybeans
2 Tbsps oil
1 Tbsp chopped Szechuan preserved vegetable or tien-tsin preserved vegetable
½ lb fresh mushrooms
½ tsp salt
½ tsp sugar

Steam fresh soybeans for 15 minutes. Or in a small saucepan cover the beans with ⅓ cup water and simmer over a very low flame for 8 minutes and drain.

Heat oil in a wok or a skillet, add preserved vegetable and mushrooms, and stir-fry 1 minute. Add soybeans, salt, and sugar. Toss and cook for 1 more minute, or until the mushroom juice is more or less evaporated. Transfer to a plate and serve hot.

Serves 4

鹽水毛豆 BOILED FRESH SOYBEANS IN THEIR PODS

These little beans bring back the bittersweet memory of my childhood days in Shanghai, sitting in front of a table full of food, looking at the big full August moon and munching on these delicious boiled beans. August Moon Festival in Shanghai was celebrated by eating all sorts of good things which were harvested just before the festival. Besides moon cakes, fresh soybeans boiled with taro roots were another must for the occasion.

Although fresh or dried soybeans are not commonly eaten in American homes, the United States is actually the world's top producer of soybeans and exports them in large quantities. If fresh soybeans are not available, they can easily be planted in home gardens, as they frequently are in China and Japan. Plant in late May or early June; the fresh tender green beans are usually ready in July.

    1 lb fresh soybeans in their pods
    4 cups water
    ½ Tbsp salt

With a pair of scissors, snip off both ends of the beans. In a saucepan bring water to a boil, add soybeans, and simmer for 5 minutes. Stir in salt and cook for another 5 minutes, or until beans become tender. Drain the water and serve them as an appetizer. The beans are eaten by putting one of the bean pods into the mouth and squeezing the beans out with the teeth; turn the bean pod around and do the same with the other end. The pod itself is not eaten.
Serves 4

雪裡紅炒豆芽 STIR-FRIED MUNG BEAN SPROUTS WITH PICKLED MUSTARD GREENS

With its refreshing taste and light crunchy texture this is just the dish for a summer day. The preserved mustard greens can be omitted if you want to cook just plain stir-fried mung bean sprouts.

    1 to 1½ lbs fresh mung bean sprouts
    ½ cup red-in-snow (pickled mustard greens)
    2 Tbsps oil
    2 slices crushed ginger or 1 tsp minced ginger
    ½ tsp salt
    ¼ cup stock
    1 tsp cornstarch dissolved in 1 Tbsp water
    1 tsp sesame oil

Rinse bean sprouts and drain, or wrap the sprouts in a dish-cloth and shake until very dry.

Rinse red-in-snow and squeeze out excess water, then chop into small pieces.

Heat oil in a wok or a skillet over a high flame. Add ginger and stir in hot oil for 5 seconds; add red-in-snow and cook for 10 seconds, then drop in bean sprouts and toss and turn everything constantly for 1 minute, sprinkling with salt while tossing. Add stock, stir in the dissolved cornstarch, then coat the sprouts with the thickened sauce. (To prevent overcooking the sprouts, the cornstarch can be mixed with the stock beforehand.) Transfer to a plate and serve at once.
Serves 4

BEAN SPROUTS STIR-FRIED WITH WHEAT GLUTEN

4 oz fried wheat gluten, commercial or homemade
   (see recipe, page 166)
1 lb fresh bean sprouts
½ Tbsp Shao-sing wine, dry sherry, or sake
1 Tbsp soy sauce
¼ tsp sugar
¼ tsp salt
2 Tbsps oil
1 tsp minced ginger
¼ cup shredded scallion

Cut wheat gluten into thin strips.

Rinse bean sprouts and drain well or wrap them in a dishcloth and shake until very dry.

In a small bowl combine wine, soy sauce, sugar, and salt, and set aside.

Heat oil in a wok over high flame, add ginger and scallion, and stir-fry them in hot oil for 10 seconds. Drop in bean sprouts and gluten and toss and turn constantly for 1 minute. Add the sauce from the small bowl, blend all the ingredients thoroughly, and stir-fry everything for an additional minute. Transfer the entire contents to plate and serve.
Serves 4

STIR-FRIED SOYBEAN SPROUTS WITH BEAN CURD PUFFS

黄豆芽炒油豆腐

One can always rely on soybean sprouts. Their truly delicate taste heightens the delicious flavor of this dish. For variation, substitute ¼ cup Szechuan preserved vegetable for the bean curd puffs.

1 lb fresh soybean sprouts
8 fried bean curd puffs, commercial or homemade (see recipe, page 124)
2 Tbsps oil
3 Tbsps chopped scallion
3 Tbsps red-in-snow (pickled mustard greens) (optional)
½ tsp salt
1 Tbsp soy sauce
½ tsp sugar
½ cup stock or water

Rinse soybean sprouts and drain. Chop the sprouts coarsely or leave them whole. Dice fried bean curd puffs.

Rinse red-in-snow and squeeze out excess water, then chop into small pieces.

Heat oil in a wok or a skillet over a medium flame, drop in scallion, and stir and cook for 1 minute. Add red-in-snow and bean sprouts, then toss and cook for about 30 seconds. Stir in salt, soy sauce, sugar, and stock; mix in the bean curd puffs last and simmer covered for 3 minutes. Serve hot.
Serves 4

CAULIFLOWER AND BEAN CURD STICKS

½ lb cauliflower
½ cup oil
2 oz bean curd sticks, broken into 2-inch sections
2 scallions, shredded
¼ tsp salt
½ Tbsp Shao-sing wine, dry sherry, or sake
1 Tbsp oyster sauce
1 Tbsp soy sauce
½ tsp sugar
½ cup stock
1 tsp cornstarch dissolved in 1 Tbsp water

Rinse cauliflower, and cut the flowery part into 1½-inch pieces. Split coarse stems.

Heat oil in a wok over high flame. Drop in bean curd sticks, 4 or 5 pieces at a time, and fry 2 seconds, or until they puff up but do not burn. Remove quickly and drain. Soak the fried bean curd sticks in hot water for 5 minutes, or until they become soft. Rinse with warm water to remove excess oil.

Empty all but 1 Tbsp oil from wok. Add scallions, cauliflower, and salt, and stir-fry for 1 minute. Add wine, oyster sauce, soy sauce, sugar, bean curd sticks and stock; blend the ingredients and cover wok. Cook for 3 minutes. Uncover pan, stir in dissolved cornstarch, and mix thoroughly. When sauce becomes thick, transfer cauliflower and bean sticks to plate and serve hot.
Serves 4

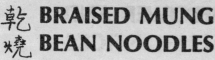

BRAISED MUNG BEAN NOODLES

Mung bean noodles are usually eaten with rice as an accompaniment and are seldom served alone. This dish is easy to prepare and very tasty.

Mung bean sheets can also be cooked the same way. Soak 4 pieces of mung bean sheets in hot water for 30 minutes, cut into 1-inch strips, and use in place of mung bean noodles.

> 2 oz dried mung bean noodles
> 1 oz Szechuan preserved vegetable
> 2 Tbsps oil
> 2 Tbsps chopped scallion
> 1 Tbsp soy sauce
> ½ tsp sugar
> 1 cup stock

Soak mung bean noodles in cold water for 30 minutes and then drain. Rinse Szechuan preserved vegetable and cut into thin slivers.

Heat oil in a wok or skillet. Add scallion and preserved vegetable, and cook for 10 seconds. Then add the noodles, soy sauce, sugar, and stock, cover pan, and simmer for 5 minutes. Remove from flame and let noodles stand in the covered pan for 10 minutes. Uncover, transfer to a plate, and serve hot or cold.
Serves 4

BRAISED CHINESE RADISH

This dish can be prepared in advance and reheated.

    1 lb Chinese radish or icicle radish
    1 leek or 3 scallions
    2 Tbsps oil
    4 slices ginger, about 1 inch in diameter
    1 Tbsp ground brown bean paste
    ½ Tbsp Shao-sing wine, dry sherry, or sake
    1 tsp sugar
    1 Tbsp soy sauce
    Dash white pepper
    1 cup stock
    1 tsp cornstarch dissolved in 1 Tbsp water

Peel radish and rinse with cold water. Split radish lengthwise into thick 1-inch strips, then roll cut the strips diagonally into pieces about 1½ inches long.

Wash leek thoroughly to rinse off sand and cut diagonally into 1-inch pieces.

Set a wok or a heavy saucepan over a moderate flame and add oil. When oil is hot, drop in leek, ginger, bean paste, and radish, and stir-fry 1 minute. Add wine, sugar, soy sauce, pepper, and stock, blend the ingredients, and cover pan and simmer over a low flame for 30 minutes or until tender. Uncover pan and thicken sauce with dissolved cornstarch. Serve hot.

Serves 4

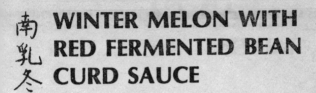

WINTER MELON WITH RED FERMENTED BEAN CURD SAUCE

One ounce of dried bean curd sticks may be added to this dish to add extra texture. Prepare bean curd sticks the same way as for Cauliflower and Bean Curd Sticks (page 192). Add bean curd sticks at the same time stock is added.

> 1 lb winter melon
> 2 Tbsps oil
> 1 Tbsp chopped scallion
> 1 Tbsp mashed red fermented bean curd
> ½ cup stock
> ½ Tbsp soy sauce
> ½ tsp sugar

Remove skin and seeds from winter melon; cut into slices ½ inch thick by 1 inch wide by 2 inches long.

Heat oil in a wok or a saucepan over a moderate flame. Add chopped scallion and cook for 5 seconds, then add fermented bean curd and stir a few times. Add winter melon, stock, soy sauce, and sugar, and stir and blend the ingredients evenly. Cover pan and simmer for 5 minutes. Uncover pan and transfer contents to a plate and serve hot.

Serves 4

紅燒冬瓜 RED-COOKED WINTER MELON OR ZUCCHINI

1 lb winter melon or zucchini
2 Tbsps oil
1 tsp minced ginger
1 tsp minced garlic
2 Tbsps chopped scallion
1 tsp curry powder (optional)
½ cup stock
¼ tsp salt (½ tsp if curry powder is used)
½ tsp sugar
2 Tbsps soy sauce (1 Tbsp if curry powder is used)
1 tsp cornstarch dissolved in 1 Tbsp water

Remove skin and seeds from winter melon and cut into 1½-inch squares, about ½ inch thick. Blanch melon in 4 cups boiling water for 3 minutes and drain. If zucchini is used, leave the skin on, cut in same manner, and omit blanching.

Heat oil in a saucepan over a medium flame, stir in ginger, garlic, scallions, and curry powder; cook for 10 seconds. Add stock, salt, sugar, soy sauce, and melon and cook and stir for 2 minutes or until winter melon becomes soft but not mushy. (If zucchini is used, cover and simmer for 2 minutes only.) Thicken sauce with dissolved cornstarch, transfer to a plate and serve.
Serves 4

STIR-FRIED ASPARAGUS WITH FERMENTED BEAN CURD

A dish to wake up to after a long gray winter. The emerald-green asparagus brings the good news of spring, and the zesty taste of fermented bean curd and chili oil heightens your spirit. If you find fermented bean curd is not to your taste, replace it with hoisin sauce. For variation, substitute string beans for asparagus and cook 2 minutes longer.

    1 lb fresh asparagus
    2 Tbsps oil
    1 tsp minced garlic
    1 Tbsp mashed white fermented bean curd
    ¼ tsp salt
    ½ tsp sugar
    ½ cup stock or water
    ½ tsp chili oil

Snap off the tough end of each stalk of asparagus, rinse stalks well, and drain. Roll-cut each one diagonally into 2-inch pieces.

Heat oil in a wok or a skillet over a high flame, stir in garlic, and cook for 5 seconds. Add fermented bean curd and stir around in hot oil for 5 seconds to bring out the flavor. Drop in asparagus, add salt and sugar, and stir-fry for 30 seconds. Add stock, cover pan, and cook over high flame for 1 minute, or until very little liquid is left in the pan. Remove lid and blend in chili oil. Serve at once.

Serves 4

腐乳生菜 STIR-FRIED LETTUCE WITH WHITE FERMENTED BEAN CURD SAUCE

The lettuce in this recipe can be replaced with a variety of vegetables, such as string beans, broccoli, cabbage, cauliflower, asparagus, or spinach, all with slightly different cooking times to bring each to the proper consistency. Consult other recipes in this book for the proper cooking times.

The original Chinese recipe calls for Ong-choy (also called Kung-sing-tsai or "hollow stemmed vegetable"), a southern specialty which is an unusual treat that should be looked for in Chinatown markets during the summer. A water plant with wedge-shaped leaves, ong-choy grows in sections like bamboo; there are nodes on the stems, and the sections between the nodes are hollow. The ong-choy season in the States is July and August. If you are lucky enough to find it, wash it thoroughly, cut into 4-inch sections, and use it in this recipe, covering the pan and cooking 2 minutes longer.

    2 Tbsps oil
    ½ Tbsp minced garlic
    2 Tbsps mashed white fermented bean curd
    4 cups coarsely shredded iceberg lettuce
    1 tsp cornstarch dissolved in 1 Tbsp water

Set a wok over a high flame and add oil and then garlic. Cook garlic for about 5 seconds. Add fermented bean curd and stir a few times; then drop in lettuce. Toss and blend for 30 seconds, and then add dissolved cornstarch. Cook a few more seconds, and when sauce becomes thick, transfer lettuce to a plate and serve hot.
Serves 4

搶 BRAISED SPICY
津 CHINESE CABBAGE
白

- 1 lb Chinese cabbage or regular cabbage
- 4 to 6 fresh or dried chili peppers
- 3 Tbsps oil
- ½ Tbsp minced ginger
- 1 Tbsp Shao-sing wine, dry sherry, or sake
- 2 Tbsps soy sauce
- 1 Tbsp wine vinegar
- ½ tsp sugar
- ⅛ tsp toasted Szechuan peppercorn powder (see recipe, page 168) or 8 Szechuan peppercorns
- 1 tsp cornstarch dissolved in 2 Tbsps stock or water (if regular cabbage is used, omit cornstarch)
- ½ Tbsp sesame oil

Wash cabbage and cut it into 1 by 2-inch pieces.

Cut dried chili peppers crosswise into small pieces.

Set a wok or saucepan over a moderate flame and stir-fry cabbage in 2 Tbsps oil for about 1 minute, or until it becomes soft. Remove from wok.

Add the remaining 1 Tbsp oil to the wok. Add chili peppers and ginger (if Szechuan peppercorns are used, drop them in at the same time as the ginger and chili). Stir and cook the spices over moderate flame for a few seconds. Add the cabbage, wine, soy sauce, vinegar, sugar, and Szechuan peppercorn powder. Mix all the ingredients thoroughly and then thicken sauce with dissolved cornstarch. Add sesame oil, remove to plate, and serve hot.
Serves 4

乾燒筍 BRAISED BAMBOO SHOOTS

This dish is from Kiangsu Province, not Szechuan, as you might expect. You can make it as fiery as you like by increasing the chili pepper. Those who are not too keen on spicy food can substitute 1 Tbsp hoisin sauce for the chili pepper, omitting sugar.

    ½ lb fresh or canned bamboo shoots
    1 cup oil
    1 Tbsp chopped Szechuan preserved vegetable
    ½ Tbsp chili pepper paste or chopped fresh
       chili pepper
    2 Tbsps soy sauce
    1 tsp sugar
    ¼ cup stock
    1 Tbsp chopped scallion
    1 tsp sesame oil

Cut bamboo shoots into pieces 1 inch wide by 1½ inches long. Pat dry with paper towels.

In a wok heat oil until very hot and deep-fry bamboo shoots for 1 minute; remove from oil and drain.

Empty all but 2 Tbsps oil from wok, add Szechuan preserved vegetable and chili pepper or paste, and cook for 30 seconds. Add bamboo shoots, soy sauce, sugar, stock, and scallion; cover and simmer for 10 minutes. Uncover, stir in sesame oil, and transfer to plate. Serve hot or cold.
Serves 4

BRAISED MUSHROOMS AND BAMBOO SHOOTS

For variation stir-fry 2 cups sliced celery in 1 Tbsp oil for 1 minute in place of bamboo shoots.

- 12 dried Chinese mushrooms, each about 1½ inches in diameter
- 2 Tbsps oil
- ½ tsp minced ginger
- 1 Tbsp soy sauce
- ½ tsp salt
- ½ tsp sugar
- ⅔ cup stock (total when combined with the mushroom water)
- 1 cup sliced bamboo shoots, about 1 inch by 2 inches
- ½ Tbsp cornstarch dissolved in 2 Tbsps water

Soak mushrooms in 1 cup hot water for 30 minutes. Drain, saving the water. Remove tough stems and cut each mushroom in half.

Heat oil in a saucepan over a medium flame; stir in ginger and cook for 10 seconds. Add mushrooms, soy sauce, salt, sugar, and stock, and simmer covered for 15 minutes.

Add bamboo shoots to saucepan and cook for 3 minutes. If there is more than ⅓ cup of liquid left in the pan, increase heat and boil rapidly until it evaporates to ⅓ cup. Thicken sauce with dissolved cornstarch and serve.
Serves 4

BRAISED BAMBOO SHOOTS WITH PICKLED MUSTARD GREENS

A remarkable, delicate dish. Use rich stock to give extra depth of flavor. You may substitute 3 cups fresh bean sprouts for the bamboo shoots.

    ½ cup red-in-snow (pickled mustard greens)
    3 Tbsps oil
    1 cup sliced bamboo shoots
    ½ tsp salt
    ½ tsp sugar
    1 Tbsp light soy sauce
    ½ cup stock
    1 tsp cornstarch dissolved in 1 Tbsp water

Rinse the red-in-snow and squeeze out excess water by hand.

Chop coarsely and set aside.

Place a wok or skillet over a moderate flame and add 2 Tbsps oil. When oil is hot, drop in bamboo shoots and stir and cook for 1 minute. Remove bamboo shoots to a plate or a bowl. Add the remaining 1 Tbsp oil into the pan, and then red-in-snow, stirring it in the oil for a few seconds. Return bamboo shoots to wok, add salt, sugar, soy sauce, and stock, mix well, and simmer everything together for 1 minute. Add dissolved cornstarch and cook until sauce is thickened. Remove to a plate and serve hot.
Serves 4

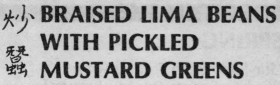

BRAISED LIMA BEANS WITH PICKLED MUSTARD GREENS

For variation, substitute fava beans or broad beans for lima beans.

 2 Tbsps oil
¼ cup red-in-snow (pickled mustard greens)
10 oz fresh lima beans or 10-oz package defrosted lima beans
½ tsp salt
 1 tsp sugar
½ cup stock
 2 Tbsps chopped scallion

Rinse red-in-snow and squeeze out excess water, then chop into small pieces.

Heat oil in a wok or a skillet, add red-in-snow, and stir for a few seconds. Drop in lima beans, blend in salt, sugar, and stock, and cover and simmer over a medium flame for 10 minutes. Uncover the wok, mix in scallion, and stir and cook until all the liquid has been evaporated. Transfer to a plate and serve either hot or cold.
Serves 4

FOREST IN THE SPRING

(Stir-Fried Bean Sprouts with Bamboo Shoots and Mushrooms)

Sprouts, bamboo shoots, mushrooms, and tree ear fungus all announce the arrival of spring, and most of the ingredients in this recipe are products of a shady forest. Hence the name is most appropriate.

> 1 cup soaked tree ears
> ½ lb fresh bean sprouts
> 5 dried Chinese mushrooms, about 1½ inches in diameter
> 3 Tbsps oil
> 3 slices ginger, about 1 inch in diameter
> 2 scallions, shredded
> ½ cup shredded bamboo shoots
> 1 Tbsp Shao-sing wine, dry sherry, or sake
> 1 Tbsp oyster sauce
> ½ tsp salt
> ¼ tsp sugar
> 1 Tbsp cornstarch dissolved in 2 Tbsps water
> ½ Tbsp sesame oil

Prepare tree ears as instructed on page 167, then cut into slivers. Set aside.

Rinse bean sprouts and drain.

Soak dried Chinese mushrooms in hot water for 30 minutes. Drain and remove stems from mushrooms, and cut each one into fine slivers. Put mushrooms in a small saucepan, add ½ cup water, cover, and simmer for 30 minutes over a slow flame. Drain.

Set a wok or skillet over a high flame and add 1 Tbsp oil. When oil is hot, drop in ginger, scallions, and bean sprouts and stir-fry constantly for about 1 minute. Remove to plate.

Add the remaining 2 Tbsps oil, swirl the oil around the pan until hot, then quickly drop in bamboo shoots, cooked mushrooms, tree ears, wine, oyster sauce, salt, and sugar. Stir all the ingredients around thoroughly and cook for 1 minute, then add bean sprouts. Mix well, then thicken with dissolved cornstarch and add sesame oil. Remove everything to a plate and serve at once.

For a variation, substitute bok choy cut into slivers for bean sprouts.
Serves 4

佛法蒲團 TEMPLE OF BUDDHA
(Braised Seaweed and Mushrooms)

In images and pictures, Buddha often appears sitting or standing on a round cushion made of grass; monks also sit on these round pads when they are meditating in the temple. In this recipe the round mushrooms stand for these pads and indicate that we are in a temple. Furthermore, since the word for "hair" and the word for "law" sound alike in Chinese, the hair seaweed can symbolize the strict "law or doctrine" to the Chinese. Use a bright colored plate to serve this dish because both hair seaweed and mushrooms are dark colored.

      ⅓ cup dried hair seaweed
     20 dried Chinese mushrooms, about 1 inch in diameter
      2 slices fresh ginger
      1 scallion
      ½ cup stock
      1 Tbsp oyster sauce
      1 Tbsp soy sauce
      ½ tsp sugar
      ¼ tsp salt
      1 tsp cornstarch dissolved in 1 Tbsp water
      ½ tsp sesame oil

Prepare hair seaweed according to instructions on page 167. Soak dried Chinese mushrooms in hot water for 30 minutes.

Remove tough stems from mushrooms and cut them in half. Put mushrooms in a saucepan, add ginger, scallion, and stock; cover and simmer for 15 minutes. Uncover, discard ginger and scallion, add oyster sauce, soy sauce, sugar, and salt, and then thicken sauce with cornstarch and add sesame oil.

Place prepared hair seaweed on a plate and arrange mushrooms on top and serve hot.

Serves 4

糖醋炒藕絲 SWEET AND SOUR LOTUS ROOTS

This recipe is indeed a case of gilding the lily—or, in this instance, the lotus root. What can be more delightful than exotic crunchy lotus roots coated with a refreshing sweet and sour sauce?

    12 oz fresh lotus root
     2 Tbsps oil
     1 tsp Szechuan peppercorns
     2 Tbsps white vinegar
    ⅓ cup stock
     1 Tbsp sugar
     1 Tbsp light soy sauce
     1 tsp cornstarch dissolved in 1 Tbsp water

Wash and peel lotus root. Cut crosswise into 2-inch sections, then cut each section lengthwise into thin strips. To prevent lotus root from discoloring, soak the cut-up lotus root in 4 cups cold water mixed with 2 Tbsps vinegar.

Heat oil and cook Szechuan peppercorns in hot oil for 1 minute or until they become dark brown. With a slotted spoon, remove peppercorns from oil and discard. Add lotus root to the peppercorn oil and mix in vinegar, stock, sugar, and light soy sauce. Toss and cook for 1 minute, then stir in dissolved cornstarch and cook until sauce becomes thick.
Serves 4

甜酸麵筋 SWEET AND SOUR FRIED GLUTEN AND CABBAGE

         6 oz fried wheat gluten, commercial or homemade
           (see recipe, page 166)
         1 Tbsp dried tree ears
         2 cups cabbage cut into 1½-inch squares
         1 Tbsp soy sauce
         2 Tbsps white vinegar
      1½ Tbsps sugar
         1 Tbsp Shao-sing wine, dry sherry, or sake
         1 cup oil
        ¾ cup stock
        ¼ cup frozen sweet peas, defrosted
        ½ Tbsp cornstarch dissolved in 2 Tbsps water

Cut gluten into 1-inch squares.

Prepare tree ears according to instructions on page 167. Cut large tree ears into small pieces.

In a small bowl combine soy sauce, vinegar, sugar, wine, and stock, and set aside.

Heat oil in a wok over a high flame. Deep-fry 6 to 8 pieces of wheat gluten for 10 seconds, remove, and drain. Repeat until all the wheat gluten is fried.

Empty all but 1 Tbsp oil from the wok and stir-fry cabbage for 1 minute. Add tree ears, green peas, and the mixture from the small bowl and bring to a boil. Thicken sauce with dissolved cornstarch, blend in fried gluten, transfer to plate, and serve at once.
Serves 4

TWO IMMORTALS IN THE APRICOT GARDEN

杏
園
花
仙

*(Fried Gluten with
Vegetables and Almonds)*

The nuts inside apricot stones resemble almonds; celery and mushrooms are the two "tasty" ingredients, and the word "tasty" in Chinese has the same pronunciation as the word "immortals." When combining almonds, mushrooms, and celery together in one plate, therefore, we have "two immortals in the apricot garden."

> 8 fried gluten balls, about 2 inches in diameter
> 10 fresh mushrooms
> ½ cup oil
> ½ cup almonds, skin removed
> 1 tsp minced ginger
> ½ cup sliced celery
> ½ tsp salt
> 1 Tbsp oyster sauce
> Dash white pepper
> ½ tsp sugar
> ½ cup stock
> 1 tsp cornstarch dissolved in 1 Tbsp of water

Prepare fried gluten balls according to recipe on page 166.

Wash in hot water to remove excess oil and cut in halves.

Rinse mushrooms and cut them into thin slices.

Heat oil in a wok over a moderate flame, drop in almonds, and fry until golden. Drain.

Empty all but 2 Tbsps oil from wok, add ginger, celery, mushrooms, and salt and stir-fry for 20 seconds. Add oyster sauce, pepper, sugar, stock, and fried gluten and blend and cook for 1 minute or until gluten becomes tender. Thicken sauce with dissolved cornstarch, add almonds, and blend. Transfer to plate and serve hot.

Serves 4

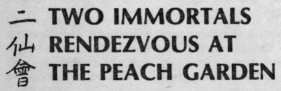

二仙會桃園 TWO IMMORTALS RENDEZVOUS AT THE PEACH GARDEN

(Walnuts Stir-Fried with Two Kinds of Mushrooms)

The Chinese word translated here as "an immortal" is a homophone for a word meaning "fresh." In this case the reference is to the fresh straw mushrooms and fresh mushrooms; walnuts are the "peaches."

> 1 cup walnuts, large pieces
> ¼ lb snow peas or ½ lb bok choy
> ½ lb fresh mushrooms
> 1 cup oil
> ½ cup fresh or canned straw mushrooms
> ½ Tbsp Shao-sing wine, dry sherry, or sake
> 1 Tbsp oyster sauce
> 1 Tbsp soy sauce
> ¼ tsp salt
> ½ tsp sugar
> ½ cup stock
> ½ Tbsp cornstarch dissolved in 2 Tbsps water
> ½ tsp sesame oil

Boil walnuts in water for 2 minutes, let cool, and remove the skins. (This last step can be omitted, but walnuts taste a bit bitter with the skin on.)

Rinse snow peas and fresh mushrooms. Snap off both tips of snow peas and remove strings from sides; cut in two diagonally, if large ones are used. Trim off tough stem ends from mushrooms and cut into slices vertically.

Heat oil in a wok and deep-fry walnuts until golden. Remove from oil with a strainer, drain, and cool.

Empty all but 1 Tbsp oil from wok. Set wok over high flame, add snow peas, stir-fry for 20 seconds, and remove to a plate. Add 2 Tbsps oil to wok, drop in fresh mushrooms and straw mushrooms, and stir-fry for 30 seconds. Add wine, oyster sauce, soy sauce, salt, sugar, and stock, and cook everything for 1 minute. Return snow peas to wok and thicken sauce with dissolved cornstarch, then drop in fried walnuts, add sesame oil, and blend evenly. Serve hot.

Serves 4

EGGS STIR-FRIED WITH PICKLED RADISH

Pickled radish is made from a large white radish which the Chinese call lo-bo and the Japanese call dai-kon. It looks like a giant icicle radish and the taste is also quite similar. Pickled radish is made by cutting up the radish into small pieces, marinating it with wine, soy sauce, sugar, and other tasty ingredients, and then drying. Since it is flavored, it can be eaten uncooked with rice or noodles as a condiment.

⅓ cup pickled radish
4 eggs, beaten
1 Tbsp chopped scallion
2 Tbsps oil

Soak pickled radish in water for 10 minutes. Rinse thoroughly with fresh water. Chop and mince.

Heat a wok or a skillet over a moderate flame, drop in minced pickled radish, and toast in an ungreased pan for 1 minute, or until it becomes dry.

In a bowl combine eggs, dried pickled radish and scallion.

Heat oil in wok or skillet. When oil is hot, pour in the egg mixture and cook and scramble until eggs become very dry.

For a variation, replace pickled radish and scallion with 1 cup stir-fried chopped Chinese chives.

Serves 4

紅燒雞蛋腐竹 BRAISED EGGS WITH BEAN CURD STICKS

This scrumptious dish is a busy cook's delight. It can be prepared a few days ahead of time and kept for a week in the refrigerator. A rich, hearty dish with all the protein you need to be healthy, it is delicious cold, at room temperature, or reheated until boiling hot. Vary it with five-spice bean curd substituted for the sticks, or add ½ cup sliced bamboo shoots.

    10 dried Chinese mushrooms
    ½   cup oil
    2   oz bean curd sticks, broken into 2-inch sectioi
    4   hard-boiled eggs
    3   Tbsps soy sauce
    1   Tbsp oyster sauce
    2   Tbsps Shao-sing wine, dry sherry, or sake
    1   tsp sugar
    3   slices ginger
    3   scallions, each cut into 3 sections
    1   cup stock (total combined with the mushroom water)
    1   tsp sesame oil

Wash mushrooms and soak them in ½ cup warm water for 30 minutes. Drain and save the water; remove tough stems and cut mushrooms into halves.

Heat oil in a wok until hot. Drop in bean curd sticks, 4 or 5 pieces at a time, and fry for 3 seconds, or until they puff up but do not burn. Remove quickly and drain. Soak fried bean curd sticks in hot water for 5 minutes, or until they become soft, then rinse with warm water to remove excess oil.

In a heavy saucepan, combine whole eggs, mushrooms, fried bean curd sticks, soy sauce, oyster sauce, wine, sugar, ginger,

scallions, and stock; simmer covered over low heat for 20 minutes. Uncover, remove and discard ginger and scallions, and then stir in sesame oil. Just before serving, cut each egg vertically into four sections and arrange them on a plate with the bean curd sticks and mushrooms. Serve hot or cold.
Serves 4

SCRAMBLED EGGS WITH FERMENTED BEAN CURD

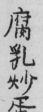

For a variation, stir-fry 1 cup shredded green pepper in 1 Tbsp oil and mix in with the egg mixture.

1 Tbsp fermented bean curd, either white or red
1 Tbsp stock or water
4 eggs, beaten
1 tsp sesame oil
Dash black pepper
2 Tbsps oil
2 Tbsps chopped scallion

In a small bowl mix fermented bean curd with stock. Stir in beaten eggs, sesame oil, and pepper.

Heat oil in a wok or a skillet over a high flame and drop in scallion; stir and cook until they become slightly brown. Add egg mixture and stir as it cooks. The consistency of the eggs should be soft and somewhat runny, but individual preference may be followed.
Serves 4

西 STIR-FRIED
施 FRESH EGGS WITH
炒 THOUSAND-YEAR EGGS
蛋

    2 thousand-year eggs
    4 fresh eggs
    2 Tbsps chopped scallion
    2 Tbsps chopped fresh coriander (optional)
    2 Tbsps chopped pickled ginger or Szechuan preserved
      vegetable (optional)
    ½ tsp salt
    Dash white pepper
    3 Tbsps oil
    ½ Tbsp soy sauce
    ½ tsp sesame oil

Scrape the mud from the thousand-year eggs by rinsing under
running water until all the mud is removed. Tap each one
against the table and remove the shell. Dice the eggs into ½-
inch pieces and set aside.

Beat fresh eggs and add scallion, fresh coriander, pickled ginger or Szechuan preserved vegetable, salt, pepper, sesame oil,
thousand-year eggs, and 1 Tbsp oil. Mix well.

Heat the remaining 2 Tbsps oil in a clean wok or a skillet over
a high flame. When oil is hot, pour in the egg mixture. With a
spatula, stir and push the mixture to the sides of the pan so
that the eggs can spread and flow to the bottom to be cooked.
When the mixture is set and dry, but not overcooked, transfer
the eggs to a plate. Pour the soy sauce over eggs and serve
at once.
Serves 4

BEAN CURD WITH SALTED EGGS

朱
砂
豆
腐

Salted eggs are a staple of the Chinese diet; the recipe on page 217 tells how to make them at home. Salted egg yolks are regarded as a delicacy; moon cakes (very sweet and rich round cakes, about 3 inches in diameter and 1½ inches thick, eaten during the Chinese Moon Festival) which have salted egg yolks in the filling, are higher priced than the kinds with other filling. Chinese usually like to hard-boil the whole egg and eat it with rice or rice porridge. The egg white, on the other hand, is salty enough so that one is adequate to accompany a couple bowls of plain rice; therefore, it is an extremely economical dish. Since salted eggs are coated with a layer of salt and ashes, it is difficult to tell a good one from a bad one. Experienced cooks claim that, if when you shake the egg near your ear, it sounds as if a firm ball were rolling around inside, then it usually is good. When high-quality salted eggs are hard-boiled the yolks become bright orange-red and ooze with oil.

> 3 salted duck eggs or 4 salted chicken eggs,
>   commercial or homemade (see recipe, page 217)
> 3 squares fresh bean curd
> 2 Tbsps oil
> ¼ tsp salt or 1 hard-boiled salted egg white,
>   finely chopped
> Dash white pepper
> 1 Tbsp light soy sauce
> 1 tsp cornstarch dissolved in 1 Tbsp water
> 1 tsp sesame oil

Scrape off the ash coating from salted eggs and rinse. Cover eggs with water and boil for 20 minutes, then soak in cold water for 10 minutes. Remove shell and egg whites and chop the yolks into fine pieces.

Rinse bean curd and mash it into a lumpy paste.

Heat oil in a wok or a skillet, add bean curd, and stir-fry for 1 minute or long enough to be heated. Add salt, pepper, soy sauce, and dissolved cornstarch and stir gently a few times. Blend in the salted egg yolks and sesame oil. Transfer to plate and serve hot.

Serves 4

SALTED EGGS

Salted eggs are also used for steaming with fresh eggs (page 223), and putting into stuffing in moon cakes, and other uses.

> 1 cup salt
> ¼ cup Shao-sing wine, dry sherry, or sake
> 1 Tbsp Szechuan peppercorns
> 10 eggs, either chicken eggs or duck eggs
> 1 large jar or a crock

Bring 5 cups water to a boil, add salt and stir until completely dissolved. Add wine and Szechuan peppercorns and let cool. Pour salt solution into the container and place the eggs into the mixture, making sure that the eggs are covered with the solution. Cover the container tightly and store it in a cool place for 4 weeks. Remove eggs from the salt solution and keep them in the refrigerator.

茶
葉
蛋

TEA EGGS

Another name for this is marbled eggs. It is so named because steeping the cracked hard-boiled eggs in a mixture of soy sauce and black tea produces a marbled effect on the egg white. Generally these eggs are not eaten with meals; they are treated as snacks or appetizers, much like potato chips for Western people. However, I think they go perfectly well with a formal dinner when cut up into small wedges and served as one of the cold dishes at the beginning of the meal.

6 eggs
1 Tbsp black tea or 3 tea bags
1 Tbsp salt
2 Tbsps soy sauce
2 whole star anise, 16 small sections
1 cinnamon stick

Hard-boil eggs in boiling water for 10 minutes. Drain off hot water and soak eggs in cold water for 15 minutes, or until they become cool. Crack shells by tapping each egg gently on all sides against a hard surface.

Place cracked eggs in a saucepan and add the rest of the ingredients and 4 cups of water. Bring everything to a boil over a medium flame, then simmer covered over a low fire for 2 hours. Soak eggs in the mixture at room temperature overnight.

Before serving, remove the shells; the whites will have a marbled pattern. Slice eggs in quarters or smaller and serve.
Serves 8 to 12

五 FIVE-SPICE
杏 EGGS
蛋

  5 medium-sized eggs, hard-boiled
  ¼ cup soy sauce
  1 tsp sugar
  2 Tbsps Shao-sing wine, dry sherry, or sake
  ½ tsp Szechuan peppercorns
  1 whole star anise
  3 slices ginger
  3 scallions

Shell eggs and place in a saucepan. Combine the rest of the ingredients with eggs and add enough water to cover. Cover pan and simmer over a low flame for 40 minutes. Turn off and let eggs stand in sauce until cool.

Cut eggs lengthwise into sections, arrange on plate and serve cold. (If a stronger flavor is preferred, strain the sauce and pour over eggs, or serve the sauce separately in a bowl.)
Serves 4 to 8

EGGS WITH SPICY SAUCE

素
魚
香
烘
蛋

1 Tbsp dried tree ears
6 eggs
1 tsp salt
½ Tbsp cornstarch dissolved in 2 Tbsps water
6 Tbsps oil
1 Tbsp soy sauce
1 Tbsp vinegar
¼ tsp sugar
1 cup stock (seasoned with salt)
1 tsp cornstarch
1 tsp minced garlic
1 tsp minced ginger
2 Tbsps chopped scallion
1 Tbsp Szechuan hot bean paste
¼ cup chopped water chestnuts
¼ cup chopped five-spice pressed bean curd (see recipe, page 123)

Prepare tree ears according to instructions on page 167.

Cut tree ears into small strips about ⅓ inch wide.

Break eggs into a bowl and add salt and the dissolved cornstarch. Beat eggs vigorously until foamy.

Set a skillet over a moderate fire and add 2 Tbsps oil. When oil is hot, pour in egg mixture. Cover pan and cook for about 2 minutes or until egg is slightly set and the bottom layer is golden brown. Uncover pan, turn the whole layer of egg over, add 2 more Tbsps oil to the pan and cook until the other side becomes golden brown. Transfer the egg to a plate and cut into rectangular pieces about 1 by 2 inches.

In a small bowl combine soy sauce, vinegar, sugar, stock, and cornstarch.

Heat 2 Tbsps oil in a wok or a skillet over high flame. Drop in garlic, ginger, scallion, hot bean paste, water chestnuts, tree ears, and pressed bean curd, and stir-fry the ingredients for 1 minute. Add soy sauce and vinegar mixture and cook and stir until the sauce becomes thick. Remove from flame and pour the whole mixture over the egg and serve.

Serves 4

STEAMED EGGS WITH SCALLION

A steamed egg custard dish is a perfect accompaniment to rice—the creamy texture makes the grains of rice easier to swallow. Chinese diners usually scoop a couple of tablespoonsful of steamed egg into their bowls of rice, and then shovel some rice mixed with egg into their mouths. This basic steamed egg dish can be varied by adding fish fillet, meat, salted eggs (page 217), or other ingredients.

To obtain a nice smooth texture, the flame should be on low and the water barely simmering. Avoid rapidly boiling water. Instead of covering the pan tightly, leave a small crack open to prevent the egg from becoming tough.

     4 eggs
     1 tsp Shao-sing wine, dry sherry, or sake
    ½ tsp salt
     1 Tbsp light soy sauce
     2 Tbsps chopped scallion
    ¼ tsp sugar
     2 cups warm stock or water
    ½ Tbsp soy sauce
     1 tsp sesame oil

In a bowl beat egg lightly not too vigorously or too long. Add wine, salt, light soy sauce, scallion, sugar, and stock, and mix well. Pour egg mixture into a shallow bowl.

Steam eggs over a low flame for 15 minutes or set the egg bowl in a pan of warm water and bake in a 350° oven for 40 minutes. When eggs are done, they should be solid and custard-like. Steam or bake longer if eggs are still runny.

Remove steamed eggs and add soy sauce and sesame oil on top. Serve at once right in the steaming dish.
Serves 4

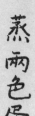

STEAMED FRESH AND SALTED EGGS

3 fresh eggs
2 salted eggs (see recipe, page 217)
1 Tbsp chopped scallion
½ tsp salt
¼ tsp sugar
½ Tbsp oil
1 cup warm stock or water

In a bowl beat fresh eggs lightly. Separate salted egg whites and yolks. Add salted egg whites to the fresh eggs and beat lightly until they are well mixed. Add scallion, salt, sugar, oil, and stock and mix well.

Cut each salted egg yolk into 4 small cubes.

Pour the egg mixture into a shallow bowl, arrange salted egg yolks neatly in it. Steam the whole thing over a low flame for 15 minutes, or until the mixture is set. Serve hot with rice.
Serves 4

EGG FOO YUNG

For a variation, 1 cup of shredded green pepper may also be added to this dish. Stir-fry green pepper together with the bean sprouts.

    3 Tbsps oil
    1 cup fresh bean sprouts or ½ cup shredded
        bamboo shoots
    3 stalks scallion shredded
    1 cup sliced fresh mushrooms
    4 large eggs
    ½ tsp salt
    Dash white pepper
    1 Tbsp soy sauce

In a skillet or a wok, heat ½ Tbsp oil over a high flame. Drop in bean sprouts and scallions and stir-fry for 10 seconds. Remove to a plate and let cool.

In the same pan, heat another ½ Tbsp oil over high flame. Stir-fry the mushrooms for 45 seconds, remove to plate and let cool.

In a bowl, beat eggs slightly with a fork. Add bean sprouts, mushrooms, salt, pepper, and soy sauce. Mix thoroughly.

Set a clean wok or skillet over a medium flame and add the remaining oil and heat. Pour in egg mixture. As soon as the bottom layer is firm, push it apart, so that the egg on top can spread and flow down to the bottom to cook. When the egg is set and dry (but not too dry), transfer the entire contents to a plate and serve at once. Avoid overcooking.

Serves 4

STEAMED THREE-COLOR EGGS

The final stage of this dish looks like a piece of modern art; colored gems of olive green, orange, brown, and white inlaid in a piece of pale yellowish marble. It is truly beautiful! Serve this dish as an appetizer at the beginning of a meal or even with drinks.

One warning: Thousand-year eggs are an accquired taste. If at first you find the taste is too strange for your palate, do try the eggs a few more times before you give them up for good.

> 2 salted eggs, commercial or homemade (see recipe, page 217)
> 2 thousand-year eggs
> 3 fresh eggs, slightly beaten
> ½ tsp sugar
> Dash white pepper
> ¼ tsp salt
> ½ Tbsp sesame oil

Scrape the ash coating from the salted eggs and rinse. Cover eggs with water and boil for 20 minutes, then soak them in cold water for 10 minutes. Remove shells and dice eggs into ½-inch pieces.

Scrape the mud from the thousand-year eggs; tap each one against a hard surface and remove shells. Dice eggs into ½-inch pieces.

Mix beaten fresh eggs with an equal amount of water and stir in sugar, pepper, salt, and sesame oil. Add diced salted eggs and thousand-year eggs and blend gently but thoroughly.

Line a 6 by 6-inch square cake pan or Corningware dish with a piece of greased waxed paper. Pour egg mixture into the cake pan, and steam in a large covered saucepan over a low flame for 20 to 25 minutes, or until the eggs are set. Remove from flame and cool.

Place a plate or a cutting board on top of the cake pan, invert the pan, and lift up, leaving the steamed eggs on the board. Remove and discard the paper. Slice the egg custard into pieces 1½ by 2 inches and about ¼ inch thick, and garnish with parsley.

Serves 4

SNACKS

If you help prepare breakfast, you get fed.
If you help in a fight you get hurt.

—*Chinese folk saying*

Snacks to the Chinese mean any kind of quick meal besides the traditional three-to-five course meals that they habitually eat twice daily. A Chinese snack ranges from a simple bowl of noodles to some elaborate delicacies. Each region has its distinctive well-known specialties. Some are noted for steamed buns, some for their won-ton and egg rolls, and others for their dumplings and noodles. I have selected a dish or two from each region for the following chapter.

Most of these delicacies probably look too complicated for a quick snack, but in China or even in Chinatowns all over the United States, they are usually sold already prepared by expert cooks whose skills have been developed just for making these dishes. For the Chinese who live in these areas, it is much more convenient to pick up these specialties already prepared than it is to cook a complete meal. However, for those who live too far away to buy these snacks ready made, selected recipes are included. All of the recipes in this chapter can be served for both informal and formal occasions.

春 SPRING ROLLS
卷 OR EGG ROLLS

Spring rolls are egg rolls; egg rolls are spring rolls. The straight translation from the Chinese to the English is "spring rolls"; just where the name "egg rolls" comes from, I really don't know. I suspect that when the Chinese first began making them in the United States, they probably used egg batter to make the wrappers. Except for the Amoy people, who include cut-up scrambled eggs as one of the ingredients in their non-fried spring rolls, as far as I know there are no other regions in China that use egg to make their wrappers or to put in their fillings.

This recipe is extremely good, but if there are any ingredients that you do not like, you can omit them. Or make up a filling of your own.

> ½ cup finely shredded soaked dried Chinese mushrooms
> 4 cups oil for deep-frying
> 2 cups fresh bean sprouts or shredded celery
> 2 cups shredded five-spiced pressed bean curd (see recipe, page 123)
> 1 cup shredded carrot, blanched
> 1 cup shredded bamboo shoots
> 1 Tbsp Shao-sing wine, dry sherry, or sake
> 2 Tbsps oyster sauce
> 1 Tbsp soy sauce
> ¼ tsp salt
> ½ tsp sugar
> Dash pepper
> ½ cup stock
> 1 Tbsp cornstarch dissolved in 3 Tbsps water
> 15 egg roll skins (commercial or homemade according to the recipe on page 232)

The filling

In a small saucepan cover shredded mushrooms with water, cover, and simmer over low flame for 15 minutes.

Heat 1 Tbsp oil in a wok over a high flame and drop in bean sprouts. Stir-fry for 15 seconds and remove to a plate. Spread bean sprouts apart so that they will not be overcooked by the heat of their own steam.

Heat 2 Tbsps oil in a wok or skillet and drop in pressed bean curd, carrot, and bamboo shoots, and stir fry for 1 minute. Add wine, oyster sauce, soy sauce, salt, sugar, pepper, mushrooms, and stock and mix everything thoroughly. Thicken sauce with dissolved cornstarch. Transfer the whole thing to a bowl or a plate and let cool. Combine bean sprouts with the filling.

Wrapping and deep-frying the rolls

Place 3 Tbsps filling in the middle of each wrapping and wrap each one into a neat roll about 4 inches long and 1 inch in diameter.

Heat the remaining oil in a wok or a deep frying pan. When oil is hot, drop egg rolls into oil one by one. Fry 4 to 5 rolls at a time, 2 minutes for each batch (for thin egg roll skins, fry for less time) or until the skin is crisp and golden brown.

Serve egg rolls whole or cut each roll into 2 or 3 even sections with a sharp knife or a pair of scissors.
Serves 6 to 8

EGG ROLL WRAPPERS

The genuine traditional Chinese egg roll wrappers are made of high gluten flour, which is very elastic. The wrappers are very thin like tissue paper. They come in two different shapes: one type is round, about 7 inches in diameter, the other type is 8 inches square.

Chinese living in the Far East never make egg roll wrappers at home because it requires years of experience and hours of practice in order to make them right. People who make egg roll wrappers for commercial use are experienced craftsmen especially trained for the task.

Thin wrappers are available in Chinatown grocery stores under the name of Shanghaiese egg roll wrappers or Doll egg roll wrappers.

This recipe can be substituted for the proper egg roll wrappers, but commercial ones are truly better.

> 4 cups all-purpose flour
> 2¼ cups water

Put flour in a mixing bowl and mix in water, ½ cup at a time until all the water is used. Beat mixture into a sticky soft dough until all the dough can be lifted out in one big handful. Cover dough with a damp cloth or put in a plastic bag and let it rest for 6 hours or overnight in the refrigerator.

Set a heavy cast-iron skillet over a low flame. When the skillet is hot, wipe the surface with a damp cloth to even out the temperature. Take the entire lump of dough in your hand and press it over the surface of the skillet. A thin layer of dough will adhere and form a thin pancake about 6 inches in diameter. Removing the remaining handful of dough and allow the pancake to bake for a few seconds. As soon as the pancake is dry, peel it off from the pan and cover it with a piece of damp cloth.

Repeat until the desired number of wrappers are made; this recipe is good for about 20 wrappers.

Serves 6 to 8

餛 WONTON SOUP
飩

The filling for wonton varies. Some Chinese vegetarians like to use soaked and chopped dried shrimp mixed with blanched spinach. If the wonton is for soup, the ingredients for the filling usually have a more powerful flavor. The following recipe is good for soup wonton only.

> 1 cake fresh bean curd, 3 by 3 inches
> 6 medium-sized dried Chinese mushrooms
> ¼ cup finely chopped preserved radish or tient-tsin preserved vegetable
> ¼ cup chopped water chestnuts
> ½ tsp salt
> Dash black pepper
> 1 Tbsp soy sauce
> ½ Tbsp sesame oil
> 1 large egg, beaten
> 30 wonton wrappers, commercial or homemade according to recipe below
> 4 cups stock
> 1 cup spinach or other green leafy vegetable

Wrap the bean curd in cheesecloth and squeeze the excess water out. Then mash the bean curd thoroughly.

Soak dried Chinese mushrooms in hot water for 30 minutes. Drain, remove stems, and chop into fine pieces.

In a mixing bowl combine mashed bean curd, mushrooms, preserved radish, water chestnuts, salt, black pepper, soy sauce, sesame oil, and egg. Mix well.

Place 1 level tsp of filling mixture in the center of each wonton wrapper. Moisten the edges of the wrapper with water. Bring the two opposite corners together by folding over the filling to form a triangle, and seal in the filling by firmly pressing around the sides of the triangle. Pull the 2 base corners of the triangle together over the filling; overlap the tips of the two corners, moisten slightly with water, and press the ends together.

Fill a large saucepan half full of water and bring to a boil; then drop in wontons. When the water boils again, add 2 cups cold water and cook wontons over a moderate flame until the water comes to a boil again. Scoop up the wontons with a strainer and drain off the water.

While the wontons are being boiled, in another saucepan bring the stock to a boil. Add the vegetable and the cooked wonton. Serve at once in a big soup bowl or individual small bowls. Serves 6 to 8

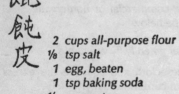 WONTON SKINS

2 cups all-purpose flour
⅛ tsp salt
1 egg, beaten
1 tsp baking soda
⅓ cup water
Cornstarch

Sift flour and salt on a board or into a large bowl. Make a hole in the middle of the flour. Pour the egg into the hole, add baking soda, mix with fingers, and gradually add the water. Mix all the ingredients until they form a stiff dough. Knead the dough for 5 to 10 minutes, set in a bowl, and cover with a damp cloth. Let set for 30 minutes to 1 hour.

Divide the dough into 2 to 3 even sections. On a surface dusted with cornstarch, roll each section one at a time into 1/16-inch thick sheets.

Cut the thin sheets into 3½-inch squares. This recipe makes about 50 wonton skins.

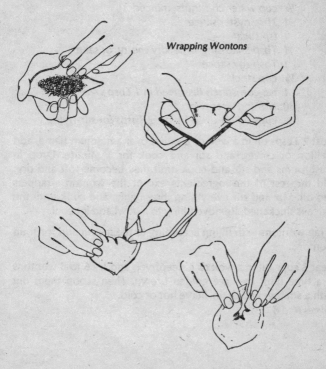

Wrapping Wontons

炸 FRIED WONTONS

餛
飩

Fried wontons are excellent to serve as canapés with drinks. They stay crisp for quite a long time, are very aesthetic, and give a touch of the exotic.

     2 Tbsps oil
    ½ cup chopped scallion or Chinese chives
     2 cups fresh mushroom, coarsely chopped
     1 square five-spice pressed bean curd, coarsely
         chopped (see recipe, page 123)
    ½ cup water chestnuts, minced
     1 Tbsp oyster sauce
     1 tsp sugar
     1 Tbsp Shao-sing wine, dry sherry, or sake
     1 Tbsp soy sauce
    ¼ cup stock
     1 tsp cornstarch dissolved in 1 Tbsp water
    30 wonton wrappers
     2 cups oil for deep frying, 2 Tbsps for stir-frying

Heat 2 Tbsps oil in a wok or a skillet over a medium flame, add scallion or chives, and stir and cook for 1 minute. Drop in mushrooms and stir and cook until they become soft and dry; add the rest of the ingredients except the wonton wrappers and oil. Mix and stir everything thoroughly, and cook until the sauce is thickened. Remove filling to a bowl and let cool.

Wrap wontons with filling according to the instruction for soup wontons.

Heat 2 cups oil in a wok or a deepfryer, and fry 6 to 8 wontons at a time until they are golden brown. Then scoop them out with a strainer and drain. Serve hot or cold.
Serves 6 to 8

SCALLION PANCAKES
(Chung Yu Ping)

When you look at this list of ingredients it may not appear to be anything very appetizing, but you will be surprised to discover how tasty simple things can really be. Scallion pancakes can be made several days ahead of time and kept in the freezer or refrigerator and reheated in 450° oven for 10 minutes. During the process of flattening out the scallion pancakes, it is very likely that the oil and the scallions will squirt out. When this happens, just roll it all back into the dough. They are good as appetizers to go with drinks or served with hot soy bean milk. (p. 247)

> 3 cups all-purpose flour
> 1 cup boiling water
> ½ cup chopped scallion
> 1½ tsps salt
> 5 Tbsps oil

Put flour in a large mixing bowl and pour in the boiling water. With a pair of chopsticks or a wooden spoon mix flour and water to form a soft dough. Knead the hot dough in the bowl or on a flat surface for 5 minutes until it is smooth. Cover dough with a damp cloth or a piece of plastic wrap in a bowl and let it set for 1 hour or longer.

Take dough out of bowl and knead for a couple more minutes on a lightly floured surface. Shape dough into a long sausage-like cylinder about 1½ inches in diameter. With a sharp knife cut dough crosswise into 8 to 10 pieces.

Roll each piece of dough into a 3- by 8-inch rectangle or into a round piece about 4 inches in diameter. Brush oil on top of each piece and sprinkle ¼ tsp salt and then ½ Tbsp chopped scallion evenly over surface. Make 3 equal folds, roll up the dough tightly like a cinnamon roll and flatten both ends of the roll with the palm of the hand. With a rolling pin roll it out again into a ¼-inch-thick pancake about 5 inches in diameter.

Set a heavy skillet over a low flame. When pan is hot, coat it with ½ Tbsp oil, put in pancake, and toast until light brown spots appear on the bottom side; then turn over and toast the other side. Or deep-fry them in hot oil for 1 minute.

Put cooked scallion pancakes on a chopping board and cut them into 4 sections. Serve hot.
Serves 4 to 6

餃子 DUMPLINGS, FRIED, STEAMED, AND BOILED

 Although I am including cooking methods for both boiled and steamed dumplings, the following recipe is really best for fried dumplings.

    1 oz dried mung bean noodles
    ½ cup chopped bamboo shoots
    ½ cup soaked tree ears
    ½ cup soaked tiger lily buds
    1 scrambled egg, chopped
    2 Tbsps chopped scallion
    1 Tbsp soy sauce
    ½ tsp salt
    ¼ tsp sugar
    ½ Tbsp sesame oil
    ⅛ tsp black pepper
    1 medium-sized egg, beaten

20 commercial or homemade dumpling wrappers
 2 Tbsps oil

Prepare tree ears and tiger lily buds according to instructions on page 167. Chop fine.

Soak mung bean noodles in hot water for 15 minutes. Drain, and with a pair of scissors, cut into short strips.

In a mixing bowl, mix all the above ingredients together except the wrappers and oil.

Wrap each dumpling by putting 1 heaping tsp filling in the center of each piece of round thin dough. Fold wrapper over into a half-moon shape and pinch a few pleats firmly along the folded edges.

Fried dumplings

Set a wok or skillet over a high flame. Coat the skillet with 1 Tbsp oil. Arrange dumplings in the pan (about 15 to 20 at a time), pour in ½ cup hot water, and cover. Cook over a medium flame for about 5 minutes or until the liquid has evaporated.

Uncover pan, add 1 Tbsp oil, and fry dumplings for 2 more minutes, or until the bottoms of the dumplings are brown.

Transfer fried dumplings carefully to a plate with the brown side up. Serve with vinegar and soy sauce.

Steamed dumplings

Line the steamer tray or a rack with a piece of damp cloth or a few big leaves of green vegetable.

Pour boiling water into a wok or a pan to reach to about 2 inches away from steamer tray or rack. Arrange dumplings on tray, cover the steamer tightly, and steam over high heat for 5 minutes.

Boiled dumplings

Fill a large saucepan with 8 to 10 cups water and bring to a boil over a high flame. Drop in dumplings and lower the flame to medium. When dumplings and the water come to a boil again, add 1 cup cold water. As soon as the water boils again, scoop up the dumplings from water with a strainer, transfer to a plate, and serve.

Serves 4 to 6

DUMPLING WRAPPERS

  2 cups all-purpose flour
  ⅔ cup boiling water for fried and steamed dumplings;
  ½ cup cold water for boiled dumplings

Put flour in a bowl and mix in water; work flour and water together until it forms a dough. Knead the dough in the bowl until it becomes smooth. Cover dough with a damp towel or a piece of plastic wrapper and let it set for at least 30 minutes.

Place dough on a floured surface and knead again for 3 minutes.

Form dough into a long sausage-like roll about 1 inch in diameter. Cut dough crosswise into 1-inch pieces. Flatten each piece with the palm of the hand and, with a rolling pin, roll it out into a thin circle about 3 inches in diameter and ⅛-inch thick.

Makes approximately 40 wrappers

薄餅 MANDARIN TORTILLAS

As wheat is a staple of northern China, the people there use flour to make all kinds of bread and buns to go with their dishes, in lieu of rice. Mandarin tortillas, or *bao-bing* in Chinese, are one type of bread which the northerners use for making a roll-up sandwich. Dishes such as Peking Duck and Mu-Shu Pork are always served with *bao-bing*, but any dish which is not too soupy can be served with it. Put 2 to 3 tablespoons of food on the tortilla, roll the whole thing up like an egg roll or an enchilada, fold one end up, and eat starting at the other end.

> 2 cups all-purpose flour
> ¾ cup boiling water
> 2 Tbsps cooking oil

Put flour in a mixing bowl; make a well in the center; then pour in the boiling water. Mix flour and water to form a soft dough with a pair of chopsticks or a wooden spoon. Knead the hot dough for 5 minutes or until it is smooth. With a damp cloth or plastic wrapping cover the dough and let it set for 30 minutes or longer.

Take dough out of bowl and knead for another minute or two on a lightly floured surface. Shape dough into a long sausage-like cylinder about 1½ inches in diameter and 14 inches in length. (For serving with Peking duck, shape dough into a cylinder 1 inch in diameter and 28 inches long.) Cut dough crosswise into 1-inch pieces, then flatten each piece with the palm of the hand into a round slice about 2 inches in diameter.

Brush one side of each slice with a thin layer of oil and then place 2 oiled sides against each other. Pair all the slices in that manner. With a rolling pin, roll each pair into thin pancakes about 6 to 7 inches in diameter (4 to 5 inches in diameter for those used with Peking duck).

Set a heavy skillet over a moderate flame. When the skillet is hot, toast the tortillas one pair at a time in an ungreased pan. As soon as a few brown spots appear on the bottom side, turn it over and toast the other side. Remove toasted tortillas from pan and separate each pair carefully. Stack tortillas on a plate and serve hot. If the tortillas are made ahead of time, they should be steamed for about 6 to 8 minutes before serving.

素 STEAMED BUNS

飽 Since steamed buns keep beautifully in the freezer, make plenty of them and when you want a few just thaw and steam them.

- ½ cup soaked tree ears
- 1 cup soaked tiger lily buds
- 6 medium-sized dried Chinese mushrooms
- ½ lb bok choy
- 2 Tbsps oil
- 1 cup chopped fresh mushrooms or ½ cup chopped straw mushrooms
- 1 tsp minced fresh ginger root
- 2 Tbsps oyster sauce
- 1 Tbsp Shao-sing wine, dry sherry, or sake
- ½ cup stock
- ½ tsp salt
- 1 Tbsp soy sauce
- ½ tsp sugar
- 1 Tbsp cornstarch dissolved in 3 Tbsps water
- 1 recipe of steamed bread dough (see recipe, page 244)

* Many Chinese living in America find ready-made plain biscuit dough a handy substitute for homemade bun dough. Biscuit dough is pre-cut to the size of a regular dinner biscuit; being smaller than the size of a bun, it takes less filling.

Prepare tree ears and tiger lily buds according to instructions on page 167. Chop fine.

Soak dried Chinese mushrooms in hot water for 30 minutes. Drain and remove stems. In a small pan simmer mushrooms with ½ cup water for 20 minutes. Chop mushrooms and set aside.

Separate bok choy stalks and wash off the dirt. Cut each stalk crosswise into 2 pieces. Place in boiling water and cook for 1 minute. Drain and rinse in cold water. Squeeze out excess water and then chop.

Set a skillet over a moderate flame and add ½ Tbsp oil. When oil is hot, add chopped bok choy. Stir-fry for 1 minute and remove to a plate.

Add another ½ Tbsp oil to the skillet and heat over moderate flame. Add mushrooms, tree ears, and tiger lily buds and stir-fry for 1 minute. Remove to a plate.

Heat the remaining 1 Tbsp oil in the skillet, add ginger and oyster sauce, and cook them in hot oil for a few seconds. Drop in bok choy, mushrooms, tree ears, and tiger lily buds and stir fry for 30 seconds. Add wine, stock, salt, soy sauce, and sugar and mix everything thoroughly. Thicken with dissolved cornstarch and remove to plate to cool.

Roll steamed bread dough into a long, sausage-shaped roll about 2 inches in diameter. Cut roll crosswise into 1½-inch sections. Flatten each section with the palm of the hand and then roll the dough out with a rolling pin to about 4 inches in diameter. The center should be a bit thicker than the edges.

Put 1 heaping Tbsp filling in the center of each wrapping. Then gather the edges of the wrapping evenly up over the filling, making a pucker at the top. Twist the peak firmly to seal. Stick a piece of waxed paper on the bottom of each bun.

Cover buns with a damp cloth and let them rise for 15 minutes. Then place buns in steamer and steam for 10 minutes over rapidly boiling water. Serve the buns hot. Cold or frozen buns can be resteamed.

Serves 6 to 8

BREAD DOUGH

This dough is used as the wrapping for steamed buns. It is also the basis for steamed bread, which in China is eaten plain.

> 2 tsps dry yeast
> ½ cup lukewarm water
> 4½ cups all-purpose flour
> 2 Tbsps sugar
> 2 Tbsps shortening
> ⅔ cup hot water

Dissolve yeast in ½ cup lukewarm water, then stir in ½ cup flour. Set aside for 15 minutes until the yeast bubbles up.

In another cup or bowl dissolve sugar and shortening in the ⅔ cup hot water and let it cool to lukewarm.

Mix 4 cups flour thoroughly with the yeast mixture and the sugar mixture, and knead for about 5 minutes or until dough is smooth. Place dough in a big bowl and cover with a damp towel or a piece of clear plastic wrap. Let it rise until it is double in size (about 2 to 3 hours).

Turn the dough onto a floured surface and knead it again for another 2 minutes until it is smooth and elastic. The dough is now ready to be made into steamed bread or used for wrapping buns.

饅 STEAMED BREAD
頭

In the northern part of China rice is not as abundant as in the south. There people use wheat flour and make it into steamed bread, baked cakes, noodles, and other foods as replacements for rice as the staple item in their diet. This recipe can be served in place of rice with stir-fried dishes.

1 recipe of steamed bread dough

After preparing the steamed bread dough recipe, divide the dough into 2 equal portions. Shape each portion into a long round roll about 1½ inches in diameter, and cut roll into 1-inch sections. Stick a piece of waxed paper on the bottom of each section; cover them with a damp cloth and let rise for 15 minutes. Then arrange the sections in a steamer and steam for 10 minutes over rapidly boiling water. Serve steamed bread hot. Leftover steamed bread can be frozen and resteamed before serving.

Serves 4 to 6

燒賣 STEAMED VEGETABLE DUMPLINGS, CANTONESE STYLE

This dish can be prepared in advance and frozen, resteamed just before serving.

- 6 oz spinach
- 1 square five-spiced pressed bean curd (see recipe, page 123)
- ½ cup soaked tiger lily buds
- ¼ cup grated carrot or water chestnuts
- 2 Tbsps soy sauce
- ½ tsp salt
- 1 Tbsp Shao-sing wine, dry sherry, or sake
- ½ Tbsp sesame oil
- 2 Tbsps rice flour
- 30 Wonton skins, commercial or homemade

Prepare tiger lily buds according to instructions on page 167. Chop fine.

Wash spinach in cold water and drain. In a large saucepan bring 6 cups water to a boil. Blanch spinach in boiling water for about 10 seconds, drain off hot water, and rinse spinach in cold water until vegetable is cold. Drain, then chop spinach into small pieces.

Cut pressed bean curd into thin pieces and then chop until pieces become very fine.

In a bowl combine spinach, pressed bean curd, tiger lily buds, grated carrot, soy sauce, salt, wine, sesame oil, and rice flour; mix all ingredients thoroughly.

Put about 1 Tbsp filling in the middle of a wrapper. Squeeze the whole thing together gently, letting the wrapper pleat around the filling naturally, making a small dumpling about 1¼ inches in diameter and 1½ inches high.

Place dumplings in steamer and steam for 5 minutes. Or place dumplings on a greased plate. Fill a large saucepan or wok with water and bring the water to a boil. Set a rack in the middle of the pan and place the plate of dumplings on a rack. Cover and steam for 5 minutes.
Serves 4 to 6

SOYBEAN MILK

Soybean milk serves an important function in the nutritional life of the Chinese; it provides them with considerable protein. In China, since cow's milk is scarce, most Chinese children are raised on soy milk. Traditionally soy milk is served hot, either sweetened with sugar or seasoned with soy sauce, vinegar, and sesame oil, as in the recipe given here. It is usually eaten as breakfast or a snack accompanying *you-tiao* (a very tasty deep-fried dough, in this book called deep-fried crullers) or *shao-bing* (a kind of baked bread, topped with sesame seeds and chopped scallion).

Today soy milk has become so popular that it is bottled and sold like regular milk. One finds chilled plain soy milk and chocolate flavored soy milk for sale—very convenient for Chinese families that have growing children. However, I still prefer my soy milk hot and sweetened with sugar or seasoned with soy sauce and some spice.

> 1 cup dried soybeans

Wash soybeans, cover with water, and soak for 6 hours or overnight.

Put soaked soybeans into a blender and add 3 cups water. Cover and blend at high speed for 1 minute.

Spread gauze over a large bowl or a saucepan, pour blended soybeans over the gauze, and drain out the milk. Gather the edges of the gauze to squeeze out the remaining milk. Discard the dregs.

Set soy milk over moderate flame and bring to a boil. Lower the flame and boil for another 2 minutes, stirring constantly.

Sweet soybean milk

To the basic recipe simply add sugar to taste.

Salty soybean milk

To the basic recipe add the following ingredients:

> 2 Tbsps finely chopped scallion
> 4 Tbsps soy sauce (more or less according to taste)
> 1 Tbsp sesame oil
> 2 Tbsps finely chopped Szechuan preserved vegetables (optional)
> Few drops hot chili oil (optional)
> Salt to taste
> 2 Tbsps vinegar (When vinegar is added, it curdles the milk; salty soybean milk is usually eaten slightly curdled. If the appearance of the soup seems too unappetizing, omit the vinegar.)

Instead of making the entire batch of soybean milk sweet or salty, it is possible to do this in individual servings by adding proportionately smaller amounts of the above ingredients to separate bowls. Traditionally soy milk is served with fried crullers.
Serves 8

油條 DEEP-FRIED CRULLERS

  3 tsp active dry yeast
  2 cups flour (pizza flour or high gluten flour)
  ⅔ tsp salt
  1 tsp baking soda
  1 tsp powdered alum
  ½ Tbsp oil
  Dry flour for dusting
  6 cups oil

Pour ⅓ cup lukewarm water into a small bowl and sprinkle dry yeast on top of the water. With a spoon stir in ⅓ cup flour; cover bowl, and let the mixture rise for ½ hour.

In a bowl dissolve salt in ⅔ cup water and then mix in the oil.

Sift remaining flour with baking soda and powdered alum into a mixing bowl. Stir in yeast mixture and then the water and oil mixture. Mix thoroughly and let rise for 30 minutes.

Place dough on a lightly floured board and knead gently 10 to 12 times. Cover dough with a piece of damp cloth or plastic wrap and let rise for about 2 hours.

Heat oil in a deep skillet over a high flame to 360°. Remove damp cloth or plastic wrap and sprinkle 1 Tbsp flour over dough. With a pastry scraper or rubber spatula, turn the dough over and sprinkle another 1 Tbsp flour over the moist surface. With a rolling pin, roll the dough into a rectangle about 4 inches wide and ½ inch thick.

Oil the blade of a sharp cleaver and cut dough into ½-inch wide strips. (Cut 6 to 8 strips at a time—always an even number.) Stack one strip of dough on top of another one; with the

blunt side of the cleaver press down the center along their length, forcing the strips to stick to each other. Lift the paired strips up by one end, which will stretch the dough a little bit as you lift it. Drop the strips into hot oil gently and fry until they turn golden brown. Drain and serve.
Serves 8

NOODLES AND
RICE DISHES

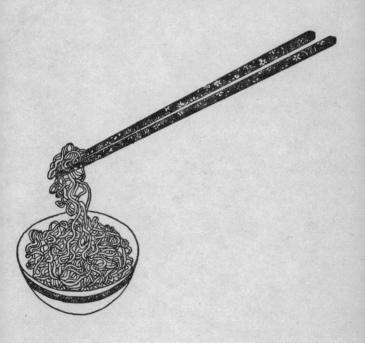

*Giving a bowl of rice to ease someone's hunger
is a good deed. Saying one word to make peace will
earn merit in the after-life.*

—"Family Teaching of
Liu Ting-gung"

NOODLES

The favorite argument about whether the Chinese learned to eat noodles from Marco Polo or the Italians were introduced to pasta by him has certainly made no difference to the Chinese nor the Italians. Whatever the true story might be, it has no effect on their passionate craving for noodles. Their united love for pasta is too strong and permanent.

The categories of Chinese noodles are extremely varied. They range from fine to coarse, wide to narrow, short to long, and chewy to soft. In addition to the endless varieties of shapes, Chinese noodles also come in numerous forms: egg noodles, which are more frequently eaten by the southerners; home-made soft noodles, which are the favorite of the northerners; very fine dried rice noodles, which are the specialty of Fukien province; and wider cut fresh rice noodles common only among the Cantonese. There is one very unique type of noodle called "hand-thrown noodles," made by starting with a lump of soft dough and then pulling and stretching the dough with both hands to its maximum length across the chest, then folding the two ends together and pulling and stretching again. Repeating the same process many times over produces very fine and even noodles. This kind of noodle is enjoyed for its chewy texture.

Besides being enormously varied, the methods of cooking Chinese noodles are also astonishingly diverse—boiling, boiling and tossing, frying, stir-frying, and steaming. Each of the Chinese regions has its own distinctive method of preparation. I have chosen a number of typical dishes representative of various methods of cooking.

蠔 OYSTER SAUCE
油 LO MEIN
撈 *(Soft Fried Noodles*
麵 *with Oyster Sauce)*

This is one of those simple and economic dishes that tastes like a million dollars. Add 1 cup stir-fried shredded cabbage or bok choy and maybe even ½ cup soaked Chinese mushrooms cut up in slivers and you have a party dish. Add mushrooms and vegetables at the same time as the scallion. The mushrooms should be boiled with ½ cup water for 10 minutes before being added to the noodles.

 ½ lb fresh Chinese noodles or ¼ lb dried Chinese
     noodles or other narrow noodles
 ½ cup finely shredded scallion
 2 Tbsps oyster sauce
 1 Tbsp soy sauce
 2 Tbsps oil
 ½ cup stock

Fill a 4-quart saucepan half full of water and bring to a boil over a high flame. Drop in noodles and bring to a boil again, loosening the noodles in water with a pair of chopsticks or a fork. When the noodles are boiling rapidly, add 1 cup cold water and bring noodles to a boil again. Cook noodles for 1 more minute. Rinse them in cold water and drain.

Set a wok or a skillet over a moderate flame and pour in oil. When oil is hot, add scallion, stirring for a few seconds. Add oyster sauce and then the noodles. Add stock, soy sauce and mix everything well. Stir and cook until most of the liquid has been absorbed. Transfer noodles to serving plate and serve hot. This dish can be prepared in advance and reheated.
Serves 4

GINGER AND SCALLION LO MEIN

½ lb fresh Chinese noodles, or ¼ lb dry Chinese egg noodles or other narrow noodles
3 Tbsps oil
1 cup finely shredded scallion
1 Tbsp finely shredded fresh ginger root
¼ tsp salt
2 Tbsps light soy sauce

Fill a 4-quart saucepan half full of water and bring to a boil over a high flame. Drop in noodles and bring to a boil again; loosening the noodles in water with a pair of chopsticks or a fork. When the noodles are boiling rapidly, add 1 cup cold water and bring noodles to a boil again. Cook noodles for 1 more minute. Rinse them in cold water and drain.

Heat oil in a wok or a big pot over a moderate flame. When oil is hot, drop in scallion and ginger and stir in oil for a few seconds: Add salt and then the noodles. Remove pot or wok from the flame, add light soy sauce, and mix everything thoroughly. Transfer noodles to a serving plate and serve at once.

Serves 4

担 担 麵 SZECHUAN-SPICY NOODLES
(Dan-Dan Mein)

This is a symphony of flavors—tangy, pungent, fragrant, garlicky, and spicy.

- 3 Tbsps soy sauce
- 1 Tbsp vinegar
- 1 Tbsp sesame oil
- 1 tsp minced garlic
- 2 Tbsps finely chopped scallion
- 1 tsp chili oil (more or less according to taste)
- 1 Tbsp oil
- 1 Tbsp finely chopped Szechuan preserved vegetable (optional)
- ½ tsp Szechuan peppercorn powder (see recipe, pg 168)
- ½ lb fresh Chinese noodles or 6 oz. dried Chinese noodles or other narrow noodles
- 2 Tbsps finely chopped roasted peanuts

In a small bowl combine soy sauce, vinegar, sesame oil, garlic, scallion, chili oil, oil, Szechuan preserved vegetable, and Szechuan peppercorn powder. Set aside.

In a large pot bring 6 to 8 cups water to a boil over a moderate flame. Drop in noodles and loosen them with chopsticks or a fork. When the noodles and water come to a boil, add 1 cup cold water. Cook noodles until the water comes to a boil again; remove noodles from heat and drain.

Pour the spicy sauce into a large serving bowl and put the cooked noodles on top of the sauce. Mix the noodles and the sauce together, sprinkle chopped peanuts on top, and serve at once.

Serves 4

拌冷燙麵 MIXED COLD NOODLES

A meal in itself, this is a very refreshing dish on a hot summer day and is ideal as a Sunday brunch or supper. It is an easy dish to make for the family, yet elegant enough to serve to company.

>   3 cups fresh bean sprouts
>   1 small cucumber
>   ¼ cup sesame seed paste or peanut butter
>   3 Tbsps soy sauce
>   1 tsp sugar
>   2 Tbsps wine vinegar
>   1 tsp hot chili oil (optional)
>   1 Tbsp sesame oil
>   ½ lb fresh egg noodles or 6 oz dried egg noodles or thin
>   spaghetti
>   1 Tbsp oil

In a saucepan bring 4 to 6 cups water to a boil over a moderate flame. Drop in bean sprouts and stir in hot water for about 5 seconds. Then drain off hot water quickly and rinse bean sprouts with cold water until they cool. Drain in colander and set aside.

Peel cucumber and cut crosswise into 2-inch sections. Cut the outer part of the sections into thin slices and discard the seeds. Shred the thin slices into slivers.

In a bowl mix sesame seed paste or peanut butter with ¼ cup warm water; stir until it becomes a thin smooth paste. Add soy sauce, sugar, vinegar, chili oil, and sesame oil.

In a large saucepan bring 8 cups water to a boil over moderate heat, drop in noodles and stir to separate. When the water boils again, add 1 cup cold water. Bring noodles and water to a boil again. Drain off boiling water and rinse noodles with cold water until cool and drain in colander. Mix 1 Tbsp oil thoroughly with noodles to prevent sticking.

Mix cucumber and bean sprouts together and put them in a serving plate. Place noodles on top of the vegetables and pour the sesame seed paste mixture over the noodles. Mix noodles, vegetables, and sauce thoroughly just before eating.

Serves 4

炸 NOODLES WITH SPICY
醬 BEAN PASTE SAUCE

麵 This popular northern noodle dish is fabulous for any time of the day. The sauce can also be served with rice. The amount of chili oil can be adjusted according to taste, or even totally omitted.

         5 dried Chinese mushrooms, about 2 inches in diameter
         3 Tbsps oil
       ½ Tbsp minced ginger
       ½ Tbsp minced garlic
         4 Tbsps chopped scallion
         1 cup coarsely chopped green pepper
         1 cup coarsely chopped five-spice pressed bean
            curd (see recipe, page 123)
         1 Tbsp Shao-sing wine, dry sherry, or sake
         3 Tbsps sweet bean paste
         1 Tbsp chili pepper paste
         2 Tbsps soy sauce
       ½ cup stock or water
         2 cups shredded cucumber or parboiled fresh bean
            sprouts
       ½ lb fresh noodles or 6 oz dried noodles or thin
            spaghetti

Soak mushrooms in ½ cup hot water for 30 minutes. Remove
and discard stems and dice the mushroom caps.

Heat oil in a wok or skillet over a high flame and stir in ginger,
garlic, scallion, and green pepper and cook for 30 seconds. Add
mushrooms, five-spice pressed bean curd, wine, sweet bean
paste, chili pepper paste, soy sauce, and stock, and stir and mix
the ingredients thoroughly. Turn the flame to low and simmer
uncovered for 5 minutes.

While the sauce is simmering, fill a large pan ⅔ full of water
and bring it to a boil over high heat. Drop in noodles and cook
for 3 to 4 minutes or until noodles are soft. Drain.

Mix cooked noodles with shredded cucumber or parboiled
bean sprouts and pour the sauce over them. The noodles can
then be divided into small portions in individual bowls.
Serves 4

SOUP NOODLES WITH EGG AND VEGETABLES

The Chinese have endless ways of preparing noodles. Here is a welcome dish for a cold winter brunch, supper, or midnight snack. There is a little bit of everything in one bowl, making for a perfectly balanced meal.

> 1 Tbsp dried tree ears
> ¼ cup tiger lily buds
> ½ lb fresh egg noodles or 6 oz dried egg noodles or thin spaghetti
> 5 cups stock
> ½ tsp salt
> 2 Tbsps oil
> ½ tsp minced ginger
> 2 cups fresh bean sprouts
> 1 cup shredded leeks or ½ cup shredded scallion
> ½ Tbsp Shao-sing wine, dry sherry, or sake (optional)
> Dash black pepper
> 2 Tbsps soy sauce
> 2 eggs, beaten
> ½ Tbsp sesame oil

Prepare tree ears and tiger lily buds according to instructions on page 167 and break into small pieces.

In a large saucepan bring 8 cups water to a boil over a moderate flame; drop in noodles and stir to separate. When the water boils again, add 1 cup cold water. Bring noodles and water to a boil again and drain noodles in a colander.

In a saucepan bring the stock to a boil; add salt.

While the broth is being boiled, heat oil over a high flame in a wok or skillet. Add ginger and leeks. Stir and cook until leeks become soft. Add tiger lily buds, bean sprouts, and tree ears and stir-fry everything for 1 minute. Add wine, pepper, and soy sauce and mix well. Pour in eggs slowly; as soon as the egg is set, remove mixture from fire. Add sesame oil.

Put noodles in a large serving bowl, pour the hot broth over them, and then add cooked vegetables and eggs. Serve at once. Serves 4

SOUP NOODLES WITH BRAISED MUSHROOMS

If you serve this noodle dish to your Chinese friends, they will eat it with great appreciation. They know how precious mushrooms are, and how elegant when blended with snow peas.

    20 dried Chinese mushrooms, about 1½ inches in
       diameter
  2½ Tbsps soy sauce
    ¼ tsp sugar
     1 tsp sesame oil
    ½ lb fresh egg noodles or 6 oz dried egg noodles
       or thin spaghetti
     1 Tbsp oil
    20 snow peas
     4 cups stock
    ½ tsp salt
       Dash of pepper

Wash mushrooms and soak them in 1 cup water for 30 minutes. Drain and save the liquid. Remove tough stems; if large mushrooms are used, cut each one in half. Put mushrooms in a small saucepan, add the mushroom liquid, 2 Tbsps soy sauce, and sugar, cover pan and simmer mushrooms over a low flame for

30 minutes. Add sesame oil. (If much liquid is left after cooking, thicken sauce with ½ tsp cornstarch mixed with 1 Tbsp water.)

In a large saucepan bring 8 cups water to a boil over moderate flame and drop in noodles and stir to separate. When the water boils again, add 1 cup cold water. Bring noodles and water to a boil again and drain noodles in a colander.

In a saucepan heat oil. Add snow peas and stir-fry for 30 seconds. Pour in stock and bring to a boil and add salt, ½ Tbsp soy sauce, and pepper.

Put noodles in a large serving bowl, pour hot soup and snow peas over them. Place cooked mushrooms on top the noodles and serve at once.

Serves 4

什 STIR-FRIED CHOP
錦 SUEY NOODLES
炒
麵

    5 medium-sized dried Chinese mushrooms
    ½ lb fresh egg noodles or 6 oz dried egg noodles or
       spaghetti
    4 Tbsps oil
    ½ cup shredded bamboo shoots or celery
    ½ cup shredded carrot
    1 cup shredded leek or onion or Chinese chives
    2 cups shredded bok choy
    ½ tsp salt
    2 Tbsps oyster sauce
    1 Tbsp soy sauce
    ½ tsp sugar
    ½ cup stock
    Dash black pepper

Wash mushrooms and soak them in ½ cup hot water for 30 minutes. Drain and save the liquid. Cut mushrooms into thin slivers and discard the stems. Put mushrooms in a small saucepan and pour in the soaking liquid. (If the liquid is not enough to cover the mushrooms, add more water.) Set pan on top of a medium flame and simmer for 15 minutes.

In a large saucepan bring 8 cups water to a boil over moderate flame and drop in noodles. Bring water and noodles to a boil again and add 1 cup cold water and stir to separate noodles. When the water comes to a boil again, remove noodles, rinse under running cold water, and drain.

Heat 2 Tbsps oil in a skillet or wok and add bamboo shoots, carrot, leek, bok choy, and salt; stir-fry everything over a high flame for 2 minutes. Add oyster sauce, soy sauce, sugar, stock, mushrooms, mushroom juice, and noodles, and stir and mix all the ingredients thoroughly. Sprinkle black pepper over noodles. Cook and stir constantly until noodles become dry. Transfer to a platter and serve at once.

Serves 4

LO HAN FRIED NOODLES

(Two-Sides-Brown Noodles)

Two-sides-brown noodles can be considered the most elegant of the noodle dishes. Velvety soft noodles are framed between two layers of crispy crust, then glazed with a luscious sauce. If the list of ingredients seems too long, you can cut back to only one kind of vegetable or one kind of mushroom and still retain the special characteristics of this excellent dish.

> ½ cup soaked tree ears
> 6 medium-sized dried Chinese mushrooms
> ½ pound fresh Chinese noodles or 6 oz dried egg
>   noodles or thin spaghetti
> 8 Tbsps oil
> ¾ tsp salt
> 1 cup celery cabbage or bok choy, or 10 snow peas
> 1 cup fresh bean sprouts
> ½ cup sliced bamboo shoots
> ⅓ cup canned straw mushrooms, cut in half
> ⅓ cup canned or 1 cup fresh mushrooms
> 1 Tbsp Shao-sing wine, dry sherry, or sake
> 1 tsp minced ginger
> 1 Tbsp soy sauce
> 2 Tbsps oyster sauce
> ½ tsp sugar
> 1 cup stock
> 1 Tbsp cornstarch dissolved in ¼ cup water

Wash dried Chinese mushrooms and soak them in ½ cup hot water for 30 minutes. Drain and remove stems. Cut larger mushrooms in half. In a small saucepan cover mushrooms with water, set over a low flame, and simmer for 20 minutes.

In a large saucepan bring 8 cups water to a boil over a moderate flame and drop in noodles. When the water and noodles come to a boil, add 1 cup cold water and stir to separate noodles. Bring everything to a boil again. Remove and drain noodles and mix in 1 Tbsp oil and ½ tsp salt.

Heat 1 Tbsp oil in a wok or a skillet over high flame. Then add celery cabbage, bok choy, or snow peas, bean sprouts, and ¼ tsp salt. Stir-fry vegetables for about 30 seconds and transfer to a plate.

Heat 2 Tbsps oil in wok or skillet over a high flame. Then add bamboo shoots, the three kinds of mushrooms, tree ears, wine, ginger, soy sauce, oyster sauce, sugar, and stock. Mix all ingredients thoroughly, cover pan, lower the flame and let cook for about 2 minutes. Uncover pan, thicken sauce with cornstarch, and then add the cooked vegetables, mixing well. Remove the entire contents from the flame and keep warm.

Add 2 Tbsps oil into a skillet (preferably a cast-iron one) and heat over a moderate flame. When oil is hot, put noodles into pan. Shake the skillet occasionally to keep the noodles from sticking, but do not stir the noodles with a spatula. Cook until the bottom layer of noodles is golden brown. Then turn the noodles over, add 2 more Tbsps oil and cook, shaking until the other side is brown also. Remove noodles gently to a serving platter, pour the vegetables over the noodles, and serve at once. Serves 4 to 6

STIR-FRIED RICE STICK NOODLES WITH VEGETABLES

菜
炒
米
粉

Rice stick noodles are the best-known Chinese food throughout Southeast Asia. They are a specialty of Fukien Province, the origin of the major Chinese emigrations which carried this dish to that part of the world.

    ½ lb rice stick noodles
    4 Tbsps oil
    1 cup shredded cabbage
    ½ tsp salt
    1 cup shredded green pepper
    1 tsp minced garlic
    ½ cup shredded scallion
    ½ cup chopped red-in-snow (pickled mustard greens)
    1 cup stock
    ½ tsp sugar
    1 Tbsp fish sauce
    Dash black pepper
    1 egg, beaten

Heat 1 Tbsp oil in a wok or a skillet over high flame. Drop in shredded cabbage, add ¼ tsp salt, and stir-fry cabbage for 2 minutes or until it becomes soft. Remove to a plate.

Heat 1 Tbsp oil in the same pan. Drop in shredded green pepper, ¼ tsp salt, and stir-fry the pepper for 1 minute. Remove to the same plate with the cooked cabbage.

Pour the remaining 2 Tbsps oil into the pan, heat over a moderate flame, then add garlic, scallion, and red-in-snow. Stir and cook for 1 minute. Then add stock, sugar, fish sauce, and pepper and bring to a boil. Then put rice stick noodles in the sauce, cover, and cook over moderate flame until all liquid is ab-

sorbed by the noodles. Uncover pan, stir in egg, and mix in vegetables. Remove to a plate and serve right away.
Serves 4

乾炒河粉 STIR-FRIED FRESH RICE NOODLES WITH BEAN SPROUTS

Fresh rice noodles are a specialty of Canton Province. They are made by steaming a rice flour batter into a large sheet about ¼ inch thick, then cutting it into strips.

> 1 lb fresh rice noodles
> 3 cups fresh bean sprouts
> 3 Tbsps oil
> 1 Tbsp brown bean paste
> 2 Tbsps stock
> 1 cup shredded scallion
> 1 Tbsp finely shredded ginger
> 2 Tbsps soy sauce
> 1 Tbsp oyster sauce
> Dash pepper
> 1 tsp sesame oil

Cut fresh rice noodles into ½-inch-wide strips. (If noodles stick together, rinse them in hot water, drain, and pat dry with paper towel.)

Wash bean sprouts with cold water and drain well. Set a wok over a high flame and heat until the wok gets very hot. Add 1 Tbsp oil, drop in bean sprouts, and stir-fry in the wok for about 20 seconds. Remove to a plate and set aside.

Heat 2 Tbsps oil in a wok over a high flame, add brown bean paste and cook in hot oil for a few seconds. Mix in stock, then drop in scallion, ginger, and then noodles. Add soy sauce and stir noodles around constantly, making sure they do not stick to the pan. Cook for 2 to 3 minutes or until they become soft and are well heated. Add oyster sauce, pepper, sesame oil, and bean sprouts, and stir-fry everything thoroughly. Transfer noodles to a plate and serve.

Serves 4

RICE

There are many varieties of rice in China and Asia, ranging through different shapes, sizes, textures, and consistencies. However, all the types that are used for plain boiled rice can be grouped into two basic varieties: long-grain and short-grain rice. Long-grain generally is very absorbent, hence it needs more water. When cooked, it fluffs up more and the grains do not stick together. The Cantonese usually prefer the long-grain rice, since they like their cooked rice a bit drier. Short-grain rice needs less water and has a softer texture and moister consistency.

I have been asked countless times by my health-conscious friends why the Chinese eat polished white rice while the rest of their diet seems otherwise so well balanced and nutritious. It is truly a contradiction, especially today when we all are trying our best to eat or serve a nutritionally sound meal. However, for the Chinese, eating polished white rice is a cultural habit—unfortunately a bad and persistent one. For centuries in China, to be able to afford to eat white rice has been a symbol of wealth; therefore it became a luxury to be enjoyed by both rich and poor. It seemed natural to the Chinese to combine the fluffy soft elegance of polished rice with their uniquely cooked dishes. As the result, we Chinese are white-rice addicts. Taking myself as an example, I would rather have a dish deficient in certain vitamins than to have to eat brown rice.

Thus, though serving white rice with Chinese dishes is more authentic, brown rice does make a healthier combination. The final choice is yours.

飯 BASIC BOILED RICE

>1 cup long-grain rice to 2 cups water
>1 cup short-grain rice to 1½ cups water

The ratio given above only serves as a guideline; the amount of water should be adjusted according to the consistency desired. In well-cooked rice each grain should be thoroughly cooked and the water fully absorbed. The result should not be too mushy nor too dry.

Traditionally the Chinese rub and rinse the rice until the water runs clear before they cook it. Since most rice that is sold in the United States has been enriched with vitamins, the rubbing and rinsing step can be omitted.

Soak rice in the correct amount of water for 30 minutes. (This is to give the rice a more fluffy texture; when you are in a hurry this step can be omitted.) Pour rice and water into a heavy saucepan with a close-fitting lid and set over a high flame. Bring rice to a rapid boil and let it boil for 3 minutes, stirring rice with a spoon once or twice. Cover saucepan tightly, turn the heat down to low, and let it cook without lifting the cover for 20 minutes. Turn off heat and let rice sit tightly covered for 15 minutes. Before serving, loosen rice with a pair of chopsticks or a fork.
Serves 4

炒
飯 FRIED RICE

    1 square five-spice pressed bean curd (see recipe,
       page 123)
    3 Tbsps oil
    2 eggs, beaten
    4 Tbsps chopped scallion
    3 cups steamed rice
    ½ tsp salt (more or less, according to taste)
Dash black pepper
    2 Tbsps soy sauce (more or less, according to taste)
    ⅓ cup defrosted frozen peas

Prepare five-spice pressed bean curd according to instructions.

Dice and set aside.

Set wok or skillet over a moderate flame and coat the pan with
1 Tbsp oil. Pour in eggs and quickly swirl around in pan; as
soon as the eggs are set, but not completely dry, turn them
over and cook for a couple of seconds longer. Remove eggs
to a plate and cut them into small pieces.

Pour the remaining oil into wok; when oil is hot, add scallion
and stir-fry in hot oil for a few seconds. Add diced pressed
bean curd and rice; stir constantly for about 2 minutes (longer
with leftover rice). Sprinkle salt and pepper while stirring the
rice. Add soy sauce and peas and stir rice around for another
minute. Last, add eggs and mix well. Remove fried rice from
pan and serve right away.
Serves 4

VEGETABLE RICE

A delicious Shanghaiese way of cooking rice. It should be served with a spicy or salty dish to contrast with the subtle taste of the rice and bok choy.

> 2 cups short-grain or long-grain rice
> 1 lb bok choy
> 3 Tbsps oil
> 1 tsp salt

Pour rice into a heavy saucepan. Wash rice a few times with cold water and drain. Add 3½ cups fresh water and soak rice for 30 minutes.

Separate boy choy stalks, rinse them well, and trim off and remove withered leaves. Dice the stalks into small pieces.

Heat oil in a wok or a skillet over a high flame. Add salt and bok choy, stir the vegetable constantly, and cook until half done—about 2 minutes. Turn off the flame and leave the vegetable in the pan, or transfer to a plate.

Set rice over high flame, bring to a rapid boil, and let it boil for about 2 minutes. Stir in cooked bok choy and the juice, if any; mix the vegetables and the rice thoroughly. Cover saucepan and turn the flame down to low, and cook for 30 minutes. Serves 4 to 6

MUSHROOM RICE

2 cups long-grain or short-grain rice
5 dried Chinese mushrooms
½ lb fresh mushrooms
2 Tbsps oil
½ cup chopped onion
1 tsp salt
½ cup fresh green peas or fresh soybeans (optional)

In a heavy saucepan, wash rice in several changes of water and drain. Add 3½ cups fresh water and soak rice for 30 minutes.

Soak dried mushrooms in ½ cup hot water for 30 minutes; drain and save soaking. Remove stems and cut mushrooms into pea-sized pieces.

Rinse fresh mushrooms and either slice or dice them. Heat oil in a wok or a skillet until very hot, then stir in onion and cook for 2 minutes or until it turns soft and slightly brown. Add fresh mushrooms and toss and cook for 2 more minutes. Turn off flame and leave mushrooms in the pan or transfer to a plate.

Set rice over a high flame, add the mushroom water, bring rice to a rapid boil, and let boil for about 2 minutes. Stir in the onion and mushroom mixture, soaked mushrooms, salt, and peas or soybeans and mix thoroughly. Cover saucepan; turn flame to low, and cook for 20 minutes. Turn off heat and let rice sit tightly covered for 15 minutes before serving.

Serves 4 to 6

鍋 RICE CRUST

巴 　Rice crust is used for sizzling rice dishes. The crust is first deep-fried until golden brown and then combined with a soupy dish. At the moment the soup and the hot rice crust come into contact they give out a sizzling sound.

> 2 cups short-grain rice
> 3½ cups water

Method one

Pour rice into a heavy saucepan or a Teflon saucepan. Wash rice a few times with cold water and drain. Add 3½ cups fresh water and set saucepan over high flame. Bring rice to a rapid boil and let it boil for about 3 minutes, stirring rice with a spoon once or twice when it is boiling. Cover saucepan tightly, turn the heat down to low, and cook for 30 minutes. After 30 minutes, tilt the saucepan on its side so that the fire can heat the sides of the pan. Turn pan around and around on its side regularly for about 1 hour.

Scoop out all the soft rice that is left, leaving a thin layer of rice crust on the pan. Heat the crust on top of a low flame until completely dry. Remove crust from pan carefully and let dry overnight, or place rice crust on a baking sheet and dry for a couple of hours in a low oven. The crust must be very dry and crisp.

Method two

Spread a layer of freshly cooked rice about 1/6 inch thick on a baking sheet; pat rice evenly and firmly. Place in a 250° oven and bake until a layer of dry crust is formed.

SWEETS

Every feast must come to an end.

—Chinese folk saying

Sweets are treated as between-meal snacks by the Chinese. Desserts are seldom eaten as one of the courses that come with a meal, as in a Western menu. However the Chinese do include a dessert of some kind in formal dinners, such as a wedding banquet or a state dinner.

Chinese sweets are just as varied, elaborate, and artful as the sweets of the Western world: some of the fancy desserts take days to prepare. When comparing Western desserts to Chinese, it is extremely difficult to offer a value judgment. I know there are people from the West who dislike all Chinese sweets; I also know some Chinese who cannot swallow a small piece of Western cake. In my opinion, it is all a matter of preference. I am including a few recipes on sweets in this book in the hope that they might sound seductive enough to arouse your interest.

SWEET SESAME DUMPLINGS

芝
蘇
湯
圓

1/3 cup black sesame seeds
1/4 cup margarine
1/2 cup sugar
1 cup glutinous rice flour
1/2 cup warm water

Toast sesame seeds in an ungreased cast-iron skillet over a low flame for about 3 minutes. Remove from flame and cool. Crush sesame seeds with mortar and pestle, or wrap in waxed paper and crush with a rolling pin.

In a bowl mix sesame seeds, margarine, and sugar together into a creamy paste. Chill the mixture in the refrigerator for at least 1 hour.

Mix glutinous flour with water and work it into a soft dough. Knead for a couple of minutes, then shape the dough into a long sausage-like roll about 1 inch in diameter. Cut dough crosswise into 1-inch pieces. Flatten each piece with the palm of the hand, put 1/2 tsp sesame seed mixture in the center, gather the edges up together, pinch tightly, and seal. Place the dumpling on the palm of one hand and place the palm of the other hand gently on top of the dumpling; roll dumpling between the palms until it becomes round. Set the dumpling on a plate and repeat until all pieces of dough are used.

Fill a large saucepan half full with water and bring it to a boil over a moderate flame. Drop in dumplings and boil for about 5 minutes. The dumplings are done when they float to the surface. Ladle the dumplings into a soup tureen along with enough water so they will not stick together and serve hot.
Serves 4 to 6

核 SWEET WALNUT SOUP

桃
酪

½ cup long-grain rice
10 dates, pitted
2 cups walnut meats
1 cup oil
⅔ cup sugar (more or less according to taste)

Cover rice with 1 cup water and soak overnight. Drain and set aside.

In a saucepan cover the dates with 1 cup water. Bring dates and water to a boil over a moderate flame, then reduce to low. Cover and simmer for about 30 minutes. Cool thoroughly and reserve the liquid.

In a large bowl cover walnut meats with very hot water and soak for 20 minutes, or boil the walnut meats over a low flame for 5 minutes. Drain and remove skins from the nuts. Pat dry with paper towels.

In a wok heat oil over a moderate flame; when oil is hot, drop in walnut meats. Fry the nuts until they become golden brown. Remove from oil and drain.

Put the rice, walnuts, dates, and the liquid into an electric blender, add 2 cups water and blend until smooth.

Pour the walnut mixture into a saucepan and add sugar and 2 more cups water. Bring to a boil over low flame, stirring constantly to prevent sticking. Cook until the mixture becomes thick. Remove from flame, pour soup into a serving bowl, and serve hot.

Serves 4 to 6

GLYZED APPLES

把
絲
苹
果

3 medium-sized apples, any variety
6 Tbsps all-purpose flour
3 Tbsps cornstarch
⅓ cup plus 1 Tbsp cold water
4 cups plus 1 Tbsp oil
⅔ cup sugar
1 Tbsp black sesame seeds, toasted (optional)
2 bowls ice water

Cut apples into quarters. Peel off skin and remove core, then cut quarters in half. Sprinkle apples with 1 Tbsp flour.

Mix a batter with remaining flour, cornstarch, and cold water. Put the apples into the batter and mix well.

Heat 4 cups oil in a wok or a deep-fryer over very high flame. When oil is very hot, drop 6 to 8 pieces of batter-coated apple into oil and fry until they turn golden brown. Remove apples and drain. Fry the rest of the apples as quickly as possible, making sure the flame is high and the oil is hot at all times.

While frying the apples, at the same time set another clean wok or a skillet over a medium flame and add sugar. When there are large bubbles, add 1 Tbsp oil along the side of the pan. Cook the sugar mixture until it turns light brown and a small drop of syrup hardens right away when dropped into ice water.

Add fried apples to the syrup and mix well. Pour the apples on a greased plate and sprinkle with black sesame seeds. Serve with ice water, into which each piece of apple is to be dipped before eating to harden the caramel.

Serves 4

DATE ROLLS

½ lb pitted dates
2 Tbsps vegetable shortening
2 Tbsps sugar
1 cup milk
⅔ cup flour
1 egg, beaten
1 tsp vanilla extract
3 cups oil

In a small saucepan cover dates with water and bring to a boil over a medium flame. Let simmer for ½ hour, then drain and mash dates until they become a paste. Set wok or skillet over a moderate flame and add shortening. When hot, put in the date paste and sugar and stir and cook the paste until most of the water is evaporated and the paste becomes dark in color. Remove to a bowl and cool.

In a mixing bowl combine milk, flour, egg, and vanilla extract and mix well.

Set a skillet over a moderate flame, coat the skillet with a little oil, then pour in ¼ cup flour mixture. Swirl around and spread the mixture into a pancake about 5 inches in diameter. As soon as the pancake is dry, put 2 Tbsps filling across the center of the pancake, fold the two sides toward the center, covering the ends of the filling, then roll the pancake up tightly and transfer to a plate. Repeat until all the date paste and the batter are used up.

Set a deep-fryer or a wok over high heat, and pour in the oil. When the oil is hot, deep-fry date rolls until light brown. Drain and cut each roll into 2 or 3 sections. Serve hot.

Serves 4 to 6

SESAME SLICES

芝
麻
鍋
炸

 ¼ cup sesame seeds
 ⅓ cup sugar
 2 eggs
 3 Tbsps milk (optional)
 1 cup cold water
 ⅔ cup flour
 ½ Tbsp sesame oil
 ¼ cup cornstarch
 4 cups oil

Toast sesame seeds in an ungreased skillet over a low flame until golden brown. Crush to a fine powder with a mortar and pestle, or wrap in waxed paper and crush with a rolling pin. Mix sesame powder with sugar and set aside.

In a mixing bowl beat eggs; then add milk and water. Mix in the flour a little at a time. Mixture should be a thin, smooth batter with no lumps.

Pour batter into a saucepan and set over a low flame. Cook and stir constantly until the mixture becomes a thick paste. Remove from flame. Grease a square cake pan with sesame oil and pour in the paste. With a rubber spatula spread the paste evenly in pan and level the top. Let cool, then chill in refrigerator for half a day.

Remove hardened paste from cake pan to a surface dusted with a little cornstarch and cut into triangular pieces. Dust with cornstarch.

Pour oil into deep-fryer or a wok and heat over a high flame until very hot. Deep-fry the cakes a few at a time until they are crisp and golden brown.

On a serving plate sprinkle some sesame and sugar mixture, and arrange fried cakes on plate. Sprinkle more sesame powder on top and serve hot or cold.

Serves 4 to 6

西米橘羹 HOT ORANGE FLOAT

½ cup pearl tapioca
¼ cup sugar
1 can mandarin oranges or 2 large oranges, peeled,
  seeded, with membrane removed
1 tsp orange extract

Soak tapioca in 1 cup water for at least 4 hours.

In a large pan combine soaked tapioca with 3 cups water and sugar. Cover pan and set over high flame. As soon as it comes to a boil, lower flame and simmer for 20 minutes, stirring occasionally to prevent sticking to the bottom of the pan. Stir in orange and orange extract and bring to a boil again.

Serve hot as a dessert.

Serves 4 to 6

八 EIGHT-TREASURE
寶 RICE PUDDING
飯

> 7 Tbsps vegetable shortening
> 1 cup prepared homemade or canned sweet red
>   bean paste (see recipe, page 285)
> 1½ to 2 cups glutinous rice
> 5 Tbsps sugar
> 4 jujubes (Chinese red dates), soaked
> Red and green candied cherries
> 4 honey dates
> 4 halves dried apricot, or 4 whole litchee nuts
> 2 halves dried pears or peaches
> 1 Tbsp candied lotus seeds (or blanched walnuts or
>   almonds)

Set wok or skillet over a moderate flame and add 3 Tbsps shortening. Then add the bean paste and stir over a low flame for about 3 minutes. Add another 2 Tbsps shortening and continue to cook for about 15 to 20 minutes, stirring constantly until the paste becomes dark in color and separates from the sides of the pan. Remove from pan to a bowl and cool.

Wash and rinse glutinous rice in cold water and drain. Put rice in a heavy saucepan and add 2¼ cups water, and bring rice to a boil over a moderate flame; let it boil for 2 minutes. Cover the pan tightly, lower the flame, and cook for 30 minutes. Remove pan from heat and let it rest for 15 minutes. Uncover pan, fluff rice with a fork, and let cool to room temperature. Mix rice with 3 Tbsps sugar and 2 Tbsps melted shortening and set aside.

Cut red dates and candied cherries in halves. Cut honey dates, apricots, and pears into strips.

Grease an 8-inch sloping bowl with shortening. Decorate the bottom and the sides of the bowl in an attractive design with the dates, candied cherries, dried fruit, and lotus seeds. Gently spread half the rice on top of the decoration. Place the red bean paste on top of the rice, then cover the red bean paste with the remaining rice. Spread rice out evenly on top to the edges of the bowl.

Place the bowl in a steamer or on a rack over a pan of boiling water. Cover and steam the rice pudding for 40 minutes to 1 hour.

The syrup

> 1½ cups water
> 3 Tbsps sugar
> 1 Tbsp cornstarch dissolved in 2 Tbsps water
> 1 tsp gwei hwa or 1 tsp grated orange rind

In a saucepan bring the water to a boil and add sugar; when sugar is all dissolved, thicken the sauce with cornstarch. When the syrup is thickened and becomes clear, add gwei hwa or orange rind.

Have a large circular serving plate ready. Remove the pudding bowl from the steamer and place the plate over it. Holding the bowl and the plate tightly, turn the whole thing over. Remove the bowl, pour the syrup over the pudding, and serve at once.

Homemade red bean paste

> 2 cups red beans
> ½ cup vegetable shortening
> ¾ cup sugar

Wash beans and soak them overnight. Cover beans with water in a saucepan, bring to a boil, and simmer over a low flame until tender. Drain off most of the water and puree cooked beans through a food mill, sieve or a food processor.

Set a wok or a skillet over a moderate flame and add shortening; when shortening is melted, add the bean paste. Cook and stir-fry constantly over a low flame, slowly adding 2 Tbsps sugar at a time. Cook until all the sugar is added and the paste becomes dark and separates from the sides of the pan. Allow to cool.
Serves 6 to 8

ALMOND FLOAT

杏仁豆腐

1 lb can mixed fruit, or mandarin oranges
1 package unflavored gelatin
1 cup boiling water
2 Tbsps sugar (for the gelatin)
½ cup cold water
½ cup cold milk
2 tsps almond extract
⅓ cup sugar (for the syrup)
1½ cups warm water

Chill canned fruit or oranges in refrigerator.

Empty gelatin into a mixing bowl and stir in boiling water and 2 Tbsps sugar until everything is dissolved and clear. Add cold water and cold milk, then stir in 1 tsp almond extract. Mix well, then pour mixture into a flat, square cake pan. The gelatin should not be more than 1 inch thick. Chill in refrigerator until it is set.

In a bowl or a measuring cup dissolve ⅓ cup sugar with 1½ cups warm water, then stir in 1 tsp almond extract. Chill syrup in refrigerator.

Cut set gelatin into 1-inch diamond-shaped pieces.

Pour syrup into a serving bowl and place gelatin into syrup gently. Then arrange fruit on top.
Serves 6 to 8

蛋 CANTONESE EGG
撻 CUSTARD TARTS

This recipe may seem very complicated, but it is simply a glorified egg custard in a flaky crust. The crust is made in a way somewhat similar to French puff pastry—pâte feuilletée, with many, many layers of thin dough. The real work in this recipe involves folding and rolling out the dough; yet this is really as simple as rolling a pie crust. Be brave and try it: you will find the result is most rewarding and satisfying.

Dough A

     10 Tbsps shortening, margarine, or vegetable lard
      2 cups all-purpose flour

Dough B

      2 cups all-purpose flour
      2 eggs, beaten
     ½ cup cold water

Custard Filling

     1½ cups sugar
     1½ cups hot water
      6 eggs, beaten

Dough A: In a large bowl cut shortening into the flour with a fork or a knife, then work with hands to form a dough. Knead dough for about 1 minute. Roll dough out into a 10 by 6-inch rectangle, wrap dough in aluminum foil, and refrigerate for 4 hours.

Dough B: Put flour into a large bowl and gradually pour in eggs and water, stirring and mixing thoroughly with a wooden spoon. Then work with hands until it becomes a soft dough and knead until smooth. Roll dough out into a 10 by 6-inch rectangle. Wrap dough in aluminum foil and refrigerate for 4 hours.

Custard Filling: In a bowl dissolve sugar in hot water and let cool. When syrup is cold, gradually pour into beaten eggs, stirring slowly until everything is well combined. Strain the egg mixture through a fine strainer or a few layers of cheesecloth.

Tarts: Unwrap chilled dough A and B, place dough A on top of dough B, and with a rolling pin roll out into a 16 by 8-inch rectangle. Dust the surface of the dough with flour, then overlap the top third and the bottom third of the rectangle by folding each toward the center of the dough. Then fold the dough in half so that it makes 6 layers. Turn dough a quarter turn, then roll it once more into a 16 by 8-inch rectangle. Dust the surface with flour and repeat the folding process as above to form 36 layers. Wrap dough in foil and chill for 2 hours.

Cut chilled dough in two sections and return half to refrigerator. Roll other half into a large piece about 1/6 inch thick. With a 2½ to 3-inch round cutter, cut the dough into round pieces. Repeat with the other half of the dough.

Place cut dough in small tart molds, pressing with fingers. Fill each mold three-quarters full of egg mixture. Bake in a 400° oven for 15 minutes or until the custard is set. Remove tarts from molds and serve hot or cold.

Serves 6 to 8

酒 FERMENTED
釀 SWEET RICE

This fermented glutinous wine rice can be eaten as a snack or mixed in with a sweet dessert such as Hot Orange Float (page 283). Wine yeast is sold in small ball form; each ball is about 1 inch in diameter and looks like a marble. It is cream colored, very light, and is available in Chinese grocery stores.

> 3 cups glutinous rice
> 1 ball wine yeast (about 2½ tsps when mashed into powder)
> ½ Tbsp all-purpose flour

Wash glutinous rice a few times in cold water until the water remains clear. Place rice in a large bowl or saucepan, cover with cold water, and soak for 6 hours.

With mortar and pestle mash the wine yeast ball into powder, or crush the ball with a rolling pin between two sheets of waxed paper. Mix the wine yeast with flour. Set aside.

Drain rice in a colander until dry. Place a piece of cheesecloth on a steamer tier, or a metal colander and spread a layer of rice about ½ inch deep. Cover and steam over rapidly boiling water for 30 minutes.

Rinse steamed rice with cold water until the rice is lukewarm; separate the grains with your hand as you rinse. Drain thoroughly. Warm a large bowl or a 6-inch square casserole with hot water and then dry it with a dish towel. Put rice in the casserole, sprinkle the wine yeast and flour mixture over the rice, and blend gently. Place a round glass about 1½ inches in diameter in the center of the casserole to make a small well, then gently pack the rice down. Cover the casserole with a lid or seal it with plastic wrap.

Wrap the casserole with a thick blanket and place in a warm, dark place for 24 hours. After the fermentation is completed, store the rice in the refrigerator, where it will keep for a long time.

花
生   # PEANUT AND SESAME
糊   # SWEET SOUP

> 1 cup roasted shelled peanuts
> ½ cup white sesame seeds
> ½ cup sugar or 1 cup honey
> ½ Tbsp cornstarch dissolved in 2 Tbsps water
> ½ cup milk (optional)

Remove the brown husks from the peanuts.

In an ungreased cast-iron skillet toast sesame seeds over a low flame until they become golden brown; transfer to a plate, spread them out, and let cool.

Put peanuts and sesame seeds in a blender, add 1 cup water and blend until the nuts turn to a smooth paste. Pour the paste into a saucepan, add sugar and 2 more cups water, and heat and stir over a low flame until soup comes to a boil. Gradually blend in the dissolved cornstarch, heat until soup thickens; then mix in the milk. Serve hot.

Here is a simplified version to use on a busy day: Mix 6 Tbsps peanut butter and 3 Tbsps tahini sesame paste with 3 cups water in a blender until smooth. Then cook with sugar and water.

For variation, substitute cashew nuts for peanuts.
Serves 6 to 8

MAIL ORDER SOURCES
FOR CHINESE INGREDIENTS

The following list of Chinese grocery stores is for the convenience of those who live in areas that have no Oriental shops. All the stores listed here carry most of the ingredients and different types of poultry that are called for in the recipes in this book and will handle mail orders.

ATLANTA
Chinatown Store, 2743 La Vista Road NE, Atlanta, Georgia 30329

BOSTON
Sun Chong Lung Co., 50 Beach Street, Boston, Massachusetts 02111

CHICAGO
Star Market, 3349 North Clark Street, Chicago, Illinois 60657

FLORIDA
Wild Oak Plantation, P.O. Box 2405, Jacksonville, Florida 32203 (Poultry only)

LOS ANGELES
Wing Chong Lung Co., 922 San Pedro Street, Los Angeles, California 90015

MINNEAPOLIS
Asia Mart, 908 Marquette Ave., Minneapolis, Minnesota 55402

NEW YORK
East Wind, 2801 Broadway, New York, New York 10025
Kam Man Food Products, Inc., 200 Canal Street, New York, New York 10013
Liang's Oriental Gifts and Grocery, Inc., 17 Saw Hill River Road (Route 9A), Elmsford, New York 10523

PHILADELPHIA
Joy Dragon Food Market, 1022 Race Street, Philadelphia,
Pennsylvania 19107

SAN FRANCISCO
The Chinese Grocer, 209 Post Street, San Francisco, California
94108
Lin Trading Co., 118 Stockton Street, San Francisco, California
94133
Metro Food Co., 641 Broadway, San Francisco, California
94133
Irving Enterprises, Inc., 681 Broadway, San Francisco, California
94133
Wo Soon Produce Co., 1210 Stockton Street, San Francisco,
California 94133

SEATTLE
Foodway Super Market and Kitchen, 200 South Jackson Street,
Seattle, Washington 98144

WASHINGTON, D.C.
Shu Ling Co., 672 North Glebe Road, Arlington, Virginia 22203

CANADA

QUEBEC
Arando Hasimoto, RR I, Thurso, Quebec Province JOX3BO
(Poultry only)

TORONTO
Wing Fong Trading Co., 136 Dundas Street West, Toronto,
Canada MSG 1C3

VANCOUVER
Wing Hing Co., Ltd., 280 East Pender Street, Vancouver, Canada
V6A 1T7

INDEX